The Total Woman Within

Anthology By Dr. Misty Beards
&
30 Contributing Co-Authors

Published by TLMM Publishing
www.tlmmpublishing.com

*Contact TLMM Publishing to connect with Authors of this Book

ISBN: 9798344799759 (Paper Back)
ISBN: 9798344867885 (Hard Back)

Printed in the United States of America

CONTENTS

CONTENTS

Forward

TLMM Editor

Apostle Janice F Thomas

Forward

Apostle Dr. Janice F. Thomas

Healing The Total Woman Within will grab every woman's heart who reads it. In your hand, you hold the tool needed for transformation. This tool transforms your inner life so you can genuinely live authentically.

We all have moments when we need to stop and examine what we harbor in our souls, such as the weight of unforgiveness, doubt, fear, hurt, pain, betrayal, guilt, rejection, and disappointments.

Life's challenges have so many of us living our lives in the shrine of other's opinions. It is only when you see yourself differently that things change. When you have healthy thoughts about your identity...others' opinions cease to be the shrine where you worship.

This may be a time of uncertainty and fear, but also an excellent opportunity to move forward in a more satisfying direction. You may be amid loss and reconstructing your life. Wherever you are in life, this book will help you assess your current state of being, including your goals, values, attitudes, behaviors, character, and desires. It will give you a spiritual compass of truth that will help you to proceed purposefully and congruently with God's will and plan for your life.

The Totally Lovin Me stories of survival and transformation will open the eyes and refresh the soul. You can only be complete if your heart is not divided between blame and unforgiveness. But when you allow faith and forgiveness to heal and liberate your soul, you will be on your way to living a Spirit-filled life of joy, peace, and contentment.

To genuinely love means to create a place for someone else and to be able to stand, make their own way, and choose a better life for themselves. Dr. Misty Beards gives each woman a place as she navigates them from the Healing Kitchen to a Healing Journey of the Soul.

Their New Life cost them their old Life...It was all Necessary!

Apostle Janice F. Thomas

A LETTER FROM THE

Lotus Flower

DR. MISTY BEARDS

A Letter From The

Lotus Flower
Dr. Misty Beards

I am the lotus, blooming in waters that may seem murky and dark. Yet, from those depths, I rise each day. Just as God created me to flourish in unlikely places, He has planted seeds of strength and beauty within you. Remember, "For I know the plans I have for you," declares the Lord, "plans to prosper you and not to harm you, plans to give you hope and a future" (Jeremiah 29:11).

Though my roots reach into muddy waters, I embrace the nourishment they provide, allowing me to grow and bloom. Like me, your experiences—even the challenges—are part of His plan, shaping you into something extraordinary. Do not fear your journey, for God is with you every step of the way. "He will be with you; he will not leave you or forsake you" (Deuteronomy 31:8).

As I unfold my petals to the light, I encourage you to open your heart to the truth of who God says you are—fearfully and wonderfully made (Psalm 139:14). Be patient with your growth, knowing that He who began a good work in you will carry it on to completion (Philippians 1:6). So, dear one, continue to rise, shine, and bloom. The world awaits your beauty, and God's love will sustain you.

With love and grace,
The Lotus-Dr. Misty Beards

Lotus Flower

TOTALLY LOVIN MY
Wisdom Pearls For The
Total Woman

TLMM Mother

Annie Craig

ABOUT THE AUTHOR

Annie Craig

Annie Craig is a native of Riceboro Georgia. She is the mother of two, grandmother of three, and a great-grandmother of 3. Annie is a retired nurse of 30+ years, and she says "Nursing is my calling from the Lord." She is the one of the mothers at River of Life Ministries and Kingdom Connections. Annie's heart is to serve the Lord, and teach the younger women and men, how to live a respectable life before the Lord.:

f Annie Craig

Wisdom & Pearls

FOR THE TOTAL WOMAN

In everyday life, every single woman faces challenges, whether it be a single woman, married with children, infertile woman, or just a single mother working two or three jobs to make ends meet. The divorced or widowed woman, a working woman in Corporate America, faces daily challenges. In the world in which we live, women wear many hats.

However, we as women cannot forget who we are as individuals. We are our unique people with dreams and goals to fulfill. We must not allow our ambitions to die within us without them fully coming to full fruition. We must allow ourselves to connect to other women who can and will lift us up. We must push each other into that next dream, goal, vision, and aspiration.

We must not give up. We must keep pushing forward even when it does not look like what we envisioned. Trusting those around us to help guide us as we glean and take pearls of wisdom from those in our best interest—especially those who want to see us succeed in every area of our lives.

Once you have done that, you will see the manifestation of things you never thought possible and can say, "I did it!" … No… "Thank you, God, WE did it!"

Annie Craig

Totally Lovin My Jesus

Author

Heather Canby Keith

ABOUT THE AUTHOR

Heather Canby Keith

I am the children's pastor of Airbrone Church and a teacher at Airborne Christian Academy. On my days off, you will find my husband and I on the baseball field cheering on our son, Jordan. My story of Totally Loving My Jesus is to encourage women to believe in the goodness of God and not to give up on the miracle you need. He will do it again and again!

TOTALLY LOVIN MY

Jesus

By Heather Canby Keith

I have witnessed the promises and goodness of my Savior in countless situations over my life. Over the years, I have been through hell and back more than once.

Growing up as a young adult, my problem was self-inflicted. However, it has been spiritual warfare as I became a woman of God. We have a relentless enemy. The beginning of John 10:10 states, "The thief comes to kill, steal, and destroy." Nevertheless, my Jesus, the only Miracle Worker, wants us to live successfully and in His will.

The final words of John 10:10 read, "My purpose is to come and give them a rich and satisfying life." To have this kind of life, we must travel the narrow road. Many do not take this path. It is a daily decision to die in the flesh and walk in the spirit. When you are living for Jesus, your prayer life must be strong.

Your prayers do not need to be louder, but you should constantly communicate with the one who paid it all on the cross for you and me. To make it in this world, you must know how to fight your battles and rise! Luke 22:46 "Rise and Pray." It took me until my late twenties to comprehend this.

I was known as the party girl after high school. Drinking numbed my pain; relationships/sex is where I got my identity, and underneath it all, I did not love or respect myself. Girls, remember your body is the Lord's temple. Protect your body, honor your body. God's power has the authority to run through your veins, but you must believe in His son to activate His power. The Holy Spirit dwells in us as believers. We can bring heaven to earth. We can become new.

I had my son Jordan when I was twenty-three. I was a single mother for over twelve years. I know what it is like to wait on the Lord. While I was waiting, God was working. Waiting builds perseverance. Waiting increases your faith. Most miracles take time to grow. We want our prayers answered instantly, but there is typically a season of waiting. I have learned the importance of not rushing but embracing those seasons.

There is a purpose in every period of life. Ecclesiastes 3:1: "There is a time for everything and a season for every activity under the heavens."

I was beginning to think that I would be single until Jesus came back to get us all. There were many lonely nights and tears, but I also remember my prayer to God. "Keep every man from me that is not my soul mate because I don't have time to waste." It was an honest, real prayer. I had already tried everything that this world could give me. While I waited, God was healing me layer by layer. When a woman bounces back from pain and trauma with Jesus by her side, her life will move forward. Shame will vanish, and the truth will cover her.

Jordan was twelve years old, and it was Easter Sunday. I can still see this sweet little face sitting beside me at church. Jordan gave his heart to Jesus in that service. We celebrated and cried together. I did not anticipate what would happen exactly seven days later, which would totally blow my mind! Jordan's biological father contacted me on a Monday evening around 5:00 PM.

After twelve years, he apologized and asked if he could begin building a relationship with Jordan. I was shocked, speechless. I remember talking to my mom and hitting my knees in prayer.

That following Tuesday, we had our women's group at church. I told God that whatever Pastor Beth speaks about, I am taking it as confirmation about Herb. "Lord, give me a sign," I prayed. That night, she said God would make crooked paths straight and give new bravery for the next season. Do what! I knew from that moment that God was a part of this reunion. As our lives unfold, hearing from God to take that next step is important. Not every road is God. Jordan met his dad on a sunny beautiful Tuesday in May. I still see him running to meet his dad on the front porch.

Life took us on a whole new path that day. Suddenly, Jordan had his mom and dad cheering him on at his baseball games. God slowly brought Herb back into Jordan's life; he lived five hours away. God is gentle and is never in a hurry. As weeks went by, Herb and I started to communicate daily. The next thing I know, we are dating and falling in love. We conquered 16 months of long distance and were married on October 19, 2019. I have learned that if you have not seen God do it, it does not mean He cannot do it!

We pray for God to use us and then get impatient when it takes longer. We want the pain to go away but do not want to put in the work. We want God to do something new in us but get scared to get uncomfortable. We pray for Jesus to send us our soul mate but have never surrendered to a single season. When Jesus is the center of your life, be ready for the unthinkable. Believe in your miracle before you are walking in your miracle. We sing the song "Break Every Chain" but start to get weary when it bends but does not break. Keep singing, sis! It will happen, and God will keep his promises.

I am totally loving my Jesus because he equips me when I feel depleted. He works in ways my mind cannot comprehend. And one thing I witnessed is if he had done it before, he would undoubtedly do it again!

Heather Canby Keith

Devotional

TOTALLY LOVIN MY

MY JESUS

"Do not conform to the pattern of this world, but be transformed by the renewing of your mind. Then you will be able to test and approve what God's will is—his good, pleasing and perfect will."

Romans 12:2 (NIV)

Devotional

Totally Lovin My Jesus

When we take our lives to Jesus, nothing is impossible for him to do. When we are open and honest, he can move. May the posture of your heart today be like Mary's. May God's will be done according to His word. Mary trusted God with an impossible situation and we can too! We are blessed when we believe!

PRAYER

Dear Jesus,

I come before You with a heart open to Your will, trusting that with You, all things are possible. Help me to surrender fully, believing in Your promises even when I cannot see the outcome. Strengthen my faith, so I can walk confidently in the path You have set before me. Let my life be a reflection of Your goodness, and may my heart be filled with trust and peace as I place everything in Your hands. I ask that Your will be done in every aspect of my life, and I thank You for the blessings that come from believing in Your word.

In Jesus' name,

Amen.

Heather Canby-Keith

Reflection
Totally Lovin My Jesus

Write a affirmation for Totally Lovin Jesus

_____

_____

_____

What steps will you take to Totally Lovin Jesus in all areas in your life?

_____

_____

_____

_____

_____

_____

_____

What does that look like?

_____

_____

_____

_____

Reflection

Totally Lovin My Jesus

List 3 take aways from this chapter.

_____

_____

_____

_____

_____

_____

Write a prayer that will help you Totally Love Jesus

_____

_____

_____

_____

_____

_____

_____

_____

Totally Lovin My Perspective

Author
Kimberly Carter

ABOUT THE AUTHOR

Kimberly Carter

Kimberly D. Carter is a seasoned Life Coach, Motivational Speaker, and Author with over 36 years of experience in Corporate America and 25 years in Ministry. As the founder and CEO of Consulting and Coaching with a Kingdom Perspective (CKP), she specializes in delivering customized administrative solutions and team-building strategies with a focus on excellence. Guided by the principle of seeking first the Kingdom of God (Matthew 6:33), Kimberly helps clients pivot perspectives, unlock their true potential, and build cohesive teams. Her approach magnifies passion, purpose, and possibilities, leading clients to achieve greatness in both ministry and the marketplace.

More importantly, Kimberly Carter is sold out to God. She is an ordained Elder of Believer's Empowerment Church and the Executive Administrator to Bishop Connie Stewart, Sr. Pastor.Her greatest joy is being the mother of a daughter who has earned her master's degree and a son who is currently enrolled in college. They are two amazing children who are charting their own path in education and entrepreneurship. By Obeying the Principles of God's Word, this humbled servant of God is called to Pivot Your Perspective!

Email: KCarter@ckpcoaching.com

Website: CKPcoaching.com

Instagram: ckpcoaching

Facebook: CKP

TOTALLY LOVIN MY

Perspective

By Kimbery D. Carter

"I Am the Pivot" …In a world filled with uncertainties and challenges, our perspectives play a crucial role in shaping our experiences and responses. Inspired by the timeless wisdom of Romans 12:2, "And be not conformed to this world: but be ye transformed by the renewing of your mind, that ye may prove what is that good, and acceptable, and perfect, will of God." I invite you to embark on a journey of transformation as we explore the power of pivoting our perspectives toward purpose.

When I was six months old, I stayed at my grandmother's house, who was babysitting me. While there, I loved looking out the window, watching people and cars go by, anticipating seeing who was coming, where you were going, and if I was going with you. I always stay "READY TO ROLL!" No matter where I was in the house, I always needed to be near the window to look out and see the world or this place of unlimited possibilities.

My grandmother took me upstairs and placed me on the bed for a nap near the window. I was not sleepy, and looking out the window was my comfort. Although there was a screen in place, I kept pushing up against the screen as cars and people passed by. The notion of fear was nowhere in my sight. My confidence and boldness did not match what was trying to stop me. The determination of my push was so great that the screen came loose, and I fell out of the second-story window of the duplex onto the sidewalk with the screen and me intact.

A neighbor across the street saw me when I hit the sidewalk and ran over to get me. I was crying uncontrollably, and they did not know the depth of pain inside of me. They called the ambulance and took me to St. Joseph Hospital for observations. Once it had been confirmed, I was ok, and it was a sigh of relief for my family. The doctor said because I was a B.I.G. baby, the fall could not damage or break me; it only knocked the wind out of me. The fact that I was a B.I.G. (Bold in God) saved my life!

Hearing this story caused me to ponder and ask the question, "Whatever happened to that B.I.G. baby?" Did she ever take the journey she saw even at six months old out of the window to unlimited possibilities? Did she continue to push with boldness, confidence, and fearlessness on her quest to discover all life had to offer? That B.I.G. baby grew up as a college graduate and married with children. Successful career in the Oil and Gas Industry. She traveled the world. Became an Ordained Elder, Entrepreneur, Author, Speaker, and Coach.

Amid success, the pain of traditions, triggers, and traumas happened. Like that B.I.G. baby, life had knocked the wind out of me in unimaginable ways. The enemy wanted to pluck up the seeds of boldness, confidence, faith, and fearlessness that was in me from my mother's womb. But purpose would not let it be so.

I remember when the P.I.V.O.T. of my healing began while sitting in a service, and the preacher spoke from John 5:6 – "When Jesus saw him lie and knew that he had been now a long time in that case, he saith unto him, wilt thou be made whole?" At that moment, I realized that the most remarkable discovery was my very own. I had reached a point where I was tired of crying and using my story to be a victim. I not only wanted change, but I wanted transformation.

As I began to navigate through my journey of discovery, I had to identify the WHY of my pain and change my way of thinking. I realized that the lens of life was always through pain and not the purpose. It was not until I had my God encounter that I understood that everything I went through was God allowed. The fact that I made it through every trial and test to be a testimony for someone else was humbling. God was the only one who turned my pain into power, but I had to be willing to do the work. In this place, I embraced the idea that I AM THE PIVOT! God wants nothing more than to give you beauty for ashes. (Isaiah 61:1-3) He was waiting for me to embrace and accept this great exchange. I invite you to do the same. I am excited to take this journey with you. Let the healing begin

Amid success, the pain of traditions, triggers, and traumas happened. Like that B.I.G. baby, life had knocked the wind out of me in unimaginable ways. The enemy wanted to pluck up the seeds of boldness, confidence, faith, and fearlessness that was in me from my mother's womb. But purpose would not let it be so.

I remember when the P.I.V.O.T. of my healing began while sitting in a service, and the preacher spoke from John 5:6 – "When Jesus saw him lie and knew that he had been now a long time in that case, he saith unto him, wilt thou be made whole?" At that moment, I realized that the most remarkable discovery was my very own. I had reached a point where I was tired of crying and using my story to be a victim. I not only wanted change, but I wanted transformation.

As I began to navigate through my journey of discovery, I had to identify the WHY of my pain and change my way of thinking. I realized that the lens of life was always through pain and not the purpose. It was not until I had my God encounter that I understood that everything I went through was God allowed. The fact that I made it through every trial and test to be a testimony for someone else was humbling. God was the only one who turned my pain into power, but I had to be willing to do the work. In this place, I embraced the idea that I AM THE PIVOT! God wants nothing more than to give you beauty for ashes. (Isaiah 61:1-3) He was waiting for me to embrace and accept this great exchange. I invite you to do the same. I am excited to take this journey with you. Let the healing begin!

As you take this time to embrace your own journey toward your healing, here are five empowerment tools to consider:

P - Pause and Reflect

The journey towards pivoting your perspective begins with a simple act: pausing to reflect. In the hustle and bustle of life, it is easy to get swept away by negativity and chaos. However, by taking a moment to pause, we create space for introspection and self-awareness.

I - Identify Limiting Beliefs

We must identify and confront the limiting beliefs that hinder our ability to see through a purpose lens. These beliefs, often ingrained through past experiences, can hinder growth and happiness. Whether it is self-doubt, fear of failure, or a cynical outlook, recognizing these limiting beliefs is the first step towards overcoming them.

V - Visualize Possibilities

With our limiting beliefs acknowledged, we must shift our focus toward possibilities. Visualization is a powerful tool that allows us to imagine beyond what we see. Through clarity and conviction, we ignite the creative spark for transformative growth.

O - Openness to New Perspectives

One of the keys to fostering a positive perspective is cultivating openness to new ideas and perspectives. Instead of clinging rigidly to our preconceived notions, we must approach life with a sense of curiosity and willingness to learn.

T - Take Inspired Action

Finally, embracing a positive perspective requires us to take inspired action toward purpose. Armed with renewed clarity and optimism, we must courageously step out of our comfort zones and pursue with unwavering determination. Each small step towards our vision reinforces our belief and propels us towards greater.

Let us remember the transformative power of perspective. By embracing the **P.I.V.O.T.** framework, we can cultivate a mindset rooted in positivity and resilience.

This is why I am Totally Lovin My Perspective!

Kimberly Carter

"The beginning of wisdom is this: Get wisdom.
Though it cost all you have, get understanding."
Proverbs 4:7 (NIV)

Reflection
Totally Lovin My Perspective

Write a affirmation for Totally Lovin Your Perspective?

_____
_____
_____
_____

What steps will you take to Totally Love Your Perspective?

_____
_____
_____
_____
_____
_____
_____
_____

What does that look like?

_____
_____
_____
_____

Reflection

Totally Lovin My Perspective

List 3 take aways from this chapter.

_____

_____

_____

_____

_____

_____

_____

Write a prayer that will help you Totally Love your Perspective

_____

_____

_____

_____

_____

_____

_____

_____

I'M TOTALLY LOVIN MY

Totally Lovin My Past

Author
Apostle Sherri Ezzell

ABOUT THE AUTHOR

Apostle Sherri Ezzell

Sherri Taylor Ezzell is a minister, author and missionary who has traveled to over 30 countries preaching the gospel, building churches and advancing the Kingdom of God. Sherri's most recent project is her e-book, For Such a Time as This: Trump, COVID-19 and The Megillah Connection. Sherri's first book, Miracle Culture, is based on her experience believing for and seeing miracles around the world. The book also includes the miracle of her son's deliverance from 10 years of heroin addiction. Sherri founded GroundBreakers Revival Hub in 2009 and launched GroundBreakers Global and Sherri Ezzell Ministries.

TOTALLY LOVIN MY

Past

By Apostle Sherri Ezzell

My son said something that hit me hard the other day. We often talk about his past drug addiction and the depths of warfare he went through before turning to Jesus for help. As many battles as I have fought, they are nothing compared to Christian's. We talked about his past when he said, "Mom, I love my past!"

As the mother of a child who fell into addiction and faced death and destruction daily, it was hard for me to digest his statement. I asked Christian to explain his meaning, and he was glad to go into more detail. He started by reviewing how he felt so ashamed during the addiction that almost took his life dozens of times. Ten years of addiction had left him with a few "dings" to his record; his name was slandered by many in our small town, and his college record was full of dropouts and failures.

The most traumatizing part of his past to me was the overdosing. I remember going to the hospital emergency room in several different cities, not knowing if he had made it. Not once did I see the shame he felt as he covered it with anger and defiance. Tears and pleading occurred in those emergency rooms, and none phased him. So, when he mentioned his shame, I was surprised.

Shame had followed me all my life. I remember feeling shame in elementary school because I never felt good enough. Dysfunction in my parents' lives resulted in me being "stuck" in the middle of a tug-of-war that I had no control over. Although I did not understand my emotions, I ran away from home in kindergarten. The feelings of shame led me to make many wrong decisions in my life; however, as my son explained his shame, I realized that he had suffered from it much more deeply than I had.

Suddenly, I understood that shame was a generational curse in my family. My mother and my father suffered the effects of shame, which were projected onto me. I vowed that my children would not experience this curse, and it came from my son. This is the trickiness of the enemy's use of generational curses: he can slide them in despite your best efforts as a parent. Although your actions can magnify generational curses, they do not come from you. They come from the enemy and run through you.

As I contemplated his original statement about loving his past, Christian explained that he had not only come to terms with his past, but he loved his past. The Lord had been dealing with Christian about what he had gone through for at least a year and had brought him to a place where he could love something he should not love: his years of pain, addiction, and, yes, shame.

I admit that I had never thought about loving my past. During our conversation, I realized overcoming regret and shame is the key to loving your past. Christian said that he stopped regretting his past when Jesus showed him that his past had made him who he is today. Without it, he would not be able to speak to addicts, love the "unlovable," or appreciate the miraculous power of Jesus. Many believers can identify with our past making us who we are today, but do we still carry regret and shame?

Ephesians 4:21-24 says, "When you heard about Christ and were taught in him in accordance with the truth that is in Jesus. You were taught, with regard to your former way of life, to put off your old self, which is being corrupted by its deceitful desires; to be made new in the attitude of your minds; and to put on the new self, created to be like God in true righteousness and holiness."

The Apostle Paul reveals in these verses that we do not just "put off" our past, but we also must be "made new" in our attitudes. We are not "new" because we took off the old. We are new when our attitude is changed. We need to see being made new as a two-step process. The first step is allowing the Lord to help us put the past behind us, and the second step is when we place our minds and our attitudes in the Lord's hands so He can make those new. The new man can love his past because his attitude and thoughts about what is behind him are made new! Shame and regret are released when this happens.

I admit that I had never thought about loving my past. During our conversation, I realized overcoming regret and shame is the key to loving your past. Christian said that he stopped regretting his past when Jesus showed him that his past had made him who he is today. Without it, he would not be able to speak to addicts, love the "unlovable," or appreciate the miraculous power of Jesus. Many believers can identify with our past making us who we are today, but do we still carry regret and shame?

Ephesians 4:21-24 says, "When you heard about Christ and were taught in him in accordance with the truth that is in Jesus. You were taught, with regard to your former way of life, to put off your old self, which is being corrupted by its deceitful desires; to be made new in the attitude of your minds; and to put on the new self, created to be like God in true righteousness and holiness."

The Apostle Paul reveals in these verses that we do not just "put off" our past, but we also must be "made new" in our attitudes. We are not "new" because we took off the old. We are new when our attitude is changed. We need to see being made new as a two-step process. The first step is allowing the Lord to help us put the past behind us, and the second step is when we place our minds and our attitudes in the Lord's hands so He can make those new. The new man can love his past because his attitude and thoughts about what is behind him are made new! Shame and regret are released when this happens.

I realized during the conversation with my son that if we are harboring feelings of regret or shame, we have not fully submitted our minds and attitudes to the Lord. This can keep a believer in Christ who has taken off the old man to still be bound in their mind. Looking back with regret on past mistakes and allowing shame to torment them, believers can enter damaging cycles of behavior and recurring problems in relationships. In effect, the past is taken off but becomes a shadow that follows us every day.

I pray that this chapter speaks to someone who is saved yet still dealing with regret and shame. These feelings are not God's will for you! Do not accept them as just "part of life" that you must deal with forever. You may have put the "old" off but go on to step two and focus on allowing the Lord to shift your mind and your attitude. You may ask how it is done. It is done through prayer and washing your mind with the Word. Memorize Ephesians 4:21-24. When thoughts of shame and regret come to you, take those thoughts captive and plunge them under the blood of Jesus! If the Lord can do this for Christian and me, He can also help you to say, **"I am totally loving my past!"**

Apostle Sherri Ezzell

"Bear with each other and forgive one another if any of you has a grievance against someone. Forgive as the Lord forgave you."

Colossians 3:13 (NIV)

Totally Lovin My Past

Write a affirmation for Totally Lovin My Past

_____
_____
_____

What steps will you take to Totally Love Your Past?

_____
_____
_____
_____
_____
_____
_____

What does that look like?

_____
_____
_____
_____

Reflection

Totally Lovin My Past

List 3 take aways from this chapter.

_____
_____
_____
_____
_____
_____
_____

Write a prayer about Totally Lovin My Past

_____
_____
_____
_____
_____
_____
_____
_____
_____

I'M TOTALLY LOVIN MY

Totally Lovin My Future

Author

Dr. Gwenette Stewart

ABOUT THE AUTHOR

Dr. Gwenette Stewart

Dr. Gwenette Stewart she is a native of Georgia. She's an author.

She's a master life coach who loves helping others. She is a mother

of five children, grandmother of twelve and she loves to serve God.

TOTALLY LOVIN MY

Future

By Dr. Gwenette Stewart

Jeremiah 29:11: "For I know the plans I have for you, Declares the Lord, plans to prosper you and not to harm you, plans to give you hope and a future."

Through our life journey, we all face tough times. These times come to make us stronger and give us a powerful testimony. It all started about a year and a half ago; I was going through a tough time in my life, and my oldest son, Terrance, would stop to check on me every day. He had started to grow closer to me, and we began to do many things together.

On April 1, 2024, I was facing a life-changing experience. This was nothing a mother would want to face. I found my thirty-four-year-old son lifeless at his home on this day. The pain that I felt was unimaginable. It felt like someone had ripped my heart out of my chest. As the days passed, I could not hear my son's voice, as he would say, "Good morning, Mama," on the other end of the phone line. That was when reality began to set in. I realized that I would not hear my son's voice anymore on the other end of the phone. Before my son's passing, I was asked to go to Destin, Florida, to the 2024 Heal Her Retreat. My son told me that he would pay for me to attend, but he did not get around to doing so.

Dr. Misty Beards, Facilitator of the Heal Her Retreat, contacted me and asked me to attend once more because she knew I needed to be there. After all, it would benefit me. I was able to attend this retreat, and it was an awesome, life-changing experience. The weekend spent at the retreat was so life-changing. I had the chance to cry out to God and release the pain and hurt that I was holding inside from the death of my first love, my son.

Words cannot explain how I felt after releasing everything weighing me down. For the first time in my life, I had the pleasure of smelling the sweet fragrance of Christ while in the presence of the Holy Spirit. This is when I started my new journey.

I remain strong by trusting in God with everything going on around me. I have learned to look at life differently. As I look forward to my future, there is room for change as I grow closer to God. I am looking forward to the work that my Father, God, has called me to do. My son's death has pushed me to another level with God. I am getting calls for me to pray for others and counsel people. I have work to do for the Lord, so giving up is not an option.

I declare and decree that my future shall be greater. I am ready to serve as the Pastor God called me to be and operate in the other gifts He has bestowed upon me. I look forward to traveling to many states to pour out the word of God to His people. I am incredibly excited about the people who will be delivered, saved, and set free through the ministry God shall birth through me.

As I open my mouth each time to preach or pray it is my prayer that the Holy Spirit will speak through me. My encouragement to everyone that is reading this is for us to live by Philippians 4:13 "I can do all things through Christ which strengthened me." What I am trying to tell you is that there is nothing that is too hard for God. I also encourage you to believe in who God says you are. He has given us promises for our lives and He also said in His words, that it is ok for us to remind Him of His promises. Live your bless life and start giving God praise for your future.

Proverbs 3:5-6 says, "Trust in the Lord with all thine heart; and lean not unto thine own understanding. In all thy ways acknowledge Him, and He shall direct thy path." He is a God that shall not lie. Find your place value in life and know your worth. Let go and let God direct your path for your future. Keep looking to the hill for which your help comes from. God is too just to make a mistake. Trust His process for your life. Whatever it is that you want to be or do in the future, just remember that if it is God's will, it will be done.

Pray for God to give you guidance over your life for your future. Do not look back too long to reflect on your past hurts, pain, disappointment, rejections, or failure but keep looking towards your calling in life. God has graced each one of us with a gift in our lives. We must tap into that special gift that He has given each of us and cause it to manifest in our lives.

Proverbs 18: 16 says, "A man's gift maketh room for Him, And bringeth him before great men." We must believe in achieving the future goals that are set up for the righteous ones. I will always hold on to this scripture: Deuteronomy 8:18, which says, "But thou shalt remember the Lord thy God, for it is He that giveth thee power to get wealth, that he may establish his covenant which he swore unto thy fathers, as it is this day." I pray that I have written something to encourage you to totally love your future. As Proverbs 4: 7 says," Wisdom is the principal thing; therefore, get wisdom: and with all, they getting get understanding." I am totally loving my Future!

Totally Lovin MY FUTURE

Dr. Gwenette Stewart

Devotional

TOTALLY LOVIN MY

FUTURE

Trust in the Lord with all your heart, and do not lean to your own understanding. In all your ways, acknowledge him, and he will direct your path.

Proverbs 3:5-6

Devotional

Totally Lovin My Future

When preparing for your future, even after a loss or transition of any kind, there are a few things that we must do. Here are some tips.

- Make a vision board.
- Spend quality time with God.
- Ask the Father for those things that you desire. Be specific!
- Give the Father praise daily, no matter what you face.
- Keep speaking life and positivity into your life.
- Trust God that he will bring your life to your prosperous place of victory.

PRAYER

Dear Heavenly Father,

I thank You for the future You have planned for me. Help me to walk forward in faith, trusting that Your plans are good and full of hope. Give me the strength to embrace the journey ahead, and help me to let go of fear and doubt. May I lean on Your wisdom, knowing that You are guiding me every step of the way. I place my future in Your hands, confident in Your love and purpose for my life. In Jesus' name, Amen.

Dr. Gwennette Stewart

Reflection  Totally Lovin My Future

Write a affirmation for Totally Lovin My Future

_____
_____
_____

What steps will you take to Totally Love Your Future?

_____
_____
_____
_____
_____
_____
_____
_____

What does that look like?

_____
_____
_____
_____

Reflection

Totally Lovin My Future

List 3 take aways from this chapter.

_____
_____
_____
_____
_____
_____
_____

Write a prayer that will help you Totally Lovin My Future

_____
_____
_____
_____
_____
_____
_____
_____

I'M TOTALLY LOVIN MY

Totally Lovin My
Treasure Within

Author

Debra Brewer

ABOUT THE AUTHOR

Debra Brewer

Debra Brewer, affectionately known as "Sunshine Queen," lives by her motto: "Making you shine." As a multifaceted professional—author, graphic designer, web designer, art therapy coach, creative branding coach, mixed media artist, and entrepreneur—Debra is dedicated to helping others uncover their God-given talents and realize their purpose. She believes that everyone has a unique calling waiting to be tapped into, empowering individuals and brands to embrace their creativity and bring their visions to life.

In her spare time, Debra shares her powerful voice through her music ministry, performing both in the Tampa Bay community and nationally. Debra is a proud mother to her daughter, her "heartbeat," who is currently in college and following her own entrepreneurial and artistic path. A passionate believer and woman of faith, Debra is committed to uplifting and encouraging others in their journeys.

www.debrabrewer.com
www.sunshinecreationsdb.com

TOTALLY LOVIN MY

Treasure Within

By Debra A. Brewer

Many of us endure feelings of inadequacy and self-doubt in silence, navigating a world where perfectionism is the standard. My own journey, much like shattered pottery, has been fragmented, flawed, and scarred by imperfections. A few years ago, I began a path of self-discovery and healing, tracing the roots of my brokenness to childhood traumas, damaged relationships, fears, depression, and an ongoing sense of not being enough.

One significant outlet on this healing path was my exploration of various art forms and a deep dive into biblical teachings and self-exploration. These practices provided me with a means to address my internal conflicts and uncover profound truths about myself.

As an artist, I invite you to join me on this quest to discover the treasure within. Imagine this journey as an evolving painting, where every brush stroke, hue, and texture symbolize a step towards healing and self-acceptance. Through the act of creation, I learned to embrace my flaws and celebrate the distinct beauty that emerges from my experiences. Come along as I illustrate a narrative of transformation and resilience, revealing the hidden treasure within the depths of my brokenness.

The Beginning of Broken Pieces:

From a young age, I was faced with trauma and dysfunction. After losing my birth mother, my sister and I were subject to abuse at the hands of my father's second wife verbally, physically, and emotionally. My father was determined to keep his family together because in the church, especially in that era, divorce was Taboo, despite the challenges that could jeopardize his career. As a pastor, my father had to maintain an appearance of normalcy, even though our home life was a living hell. I can see how the enemy seeks to destroy, particularly targeting families in ministry. We became targeted by the enemy's snare.

Due to frequent relocations required by my father's pastoral assignments every 4-6 years, I struggled to maintain long-term friendships, often leading to feelings of isolation and vulnerability to bullying. Adversities from childhood trauma extended to my eating habits, leading to enduring struggles with weight and self-worth. Comments about my appearance from a loved family member significantly affected me. My relative told me that I didn't look human, which left a scar that I wasn't able to shake.

I started to believe the lie that my weight made me unlovable; I entered relationships with low self-esteem during my late teens, a time when my depression intensified. This vulnerability made me susceptible to manipulation, deepening my loneliness and despair. My greatest wish was to feel accepted and loved.

The Cracks of Imperfection: A Journey of Struggle

The cracks in my life, once sources of shame, became more evident as I grew older. Each one marked a struggle—battles with self-doubt, depression, and the shadows of my past. These struggles deeply shaped my perception of myself and the world. I felt unworthy, often comparing myself to others who seemed to have it all together.

Raising my daughter alone was very challenging, and I focused entirely on her, setting aside my longing for companionship. I thought I was content alone until a past love reappeared, reigniting old feelings. His relentless affection swayed me despite my doubts. I soon learned that familiarity doesn't equate to a genuine spiritual connection. (He would say, Baby, pray for me, but never prayed with me or covered me in prayer) After his engagement proposal, his demeanor changed from loving to verbally hostile. I later discovered he was engaged to two other women—one in the States and another abroad. The situation grew more toxic and worsened when both women contacted me. My life was similar to a Lifetime Movie. I felt foolish, deeply betrayed, and emotionally numb, a walking zombie. My trust in others was shattered, as this person had been a friend since childhood.

I could sense demonic forces attempting to take my life. My father was en- route for a mission trip to Africa. I shared with him my burden of shame, the mistakes and compromises I had made. I was so overwhelmed I couldn't even pray. My father advised, "Just call on the name of Jesus."

I had to function for the sake of my child but was dead inside. The demonic forces would attack me again as I lay in bed. Not able to utter a word, I cried silently. Jesus, help me. Jesus, if you can hear my cry, help me!

Several women, guided by the Holy Spirit, prayed over and anointed me one evening during a choir rehearsal. That night, I was liberated from that dark spirit after a great spiritual struggle. By the next morning, I felt restored. Looking back tears well up because I know God is real! He heard my cries!

Discovering the Art of Kintsugi: Revelation of beauty in the brokenness

During my healing journey, I rediscovered my passion for art. I explored Kintsugi, a Japanese technique that mends broken pottery with gold. Inspired, I created a silhouette painting of a woman in this style. This art form, which transforms broken pieces into something more beautiful, mirrored my recovery, helping me manage emotions and gain clarity. It resonated with how God heals and enhances us with His light, turning our flaws into strengths. This artistic pursuit deepened my meditation and connection with God, reflecting His transformative impact on my life.

From Brokenness to Finding the Treasure Within

The Bible talks about moving from brokenness to uncovering essential value, often described as finding a "treasure within." Key insights are:

- ·**Restoration through Christ** (Psalm 34:18): Emphasizes God's power to heal and restore the brokenhearted.
- ·**Transformation in Christ** (2 Corinthians 5:17): Discusses how we become new creations in Christ, turning past **brokenness into hope and purpose.**
- ·**The Potter and the Clay** (Jeremiah 18:1-6) Illustrates God as a potter who reshapes and repairs us into something beautiful.
- ·**Strength in Weakness** (2 Corinthians 12:9): Explains how God's power perfects our weaknesses, turning them into strengths.
- ·**Parable of the Hidden Treasure** (Matthew 13:44): Compares the kingdom of heaven to a hidden treasure, highlighting the value of spiritual life and our relationship with God during trials.

Embracing Imperfections: A Testament to Inner Treasure

God is actively working in my life, bringing hope and joy, healing my wounds. He strengthens and illuminates my brokenness, mending it with His golden light. On this journey, I've learned to love myself, seeing my true worth through God's eyes rather than society's. He reminds me that I am fearfully and wonderfully made, cherished as the apple of His eye, and meant to live an abundant life. This understanding has empowered me to forgive and let go of unreciprocated relationships, recognizing that embracing God's love requires releasing what is not meant for me.

I am totally loving my treasure within

Debra Brewer

Devotional

TOTALLY LOVIN MY

TREASURE WITHIN

"But we have this treasure in jars of clay to show that this all-surpassing power is from God and not from us."

2 Corinthians 4:7 (NIV)

Devotional

Totally Lovin My Treasure Within

Just as Kintsugi pottery highlights brokenness as part of the beauty, God uses our struggles and imperfections to reveal the treasure He has placed within us. Embrace the treasure within you, for in Christ, our scars become a testimony of His redemptive power. We are made whole and more valuable through His love and grace.

PRAYER

Heavenly Father, I thank You for taking the broken parts of my life and using them for Your glory. Teach me to see the beauty in my journey, knowing that You are making me whole and refining the treasure within me. Let Your grace shine through every imperfection. In Jesus' name, Amen.

Debra Brewer

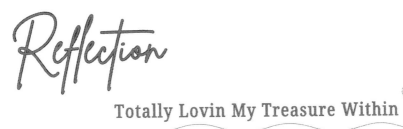

Reflection

Totally Lovin My Treasure Within

Write a affirmation to Totally Love Your Treasure within?

_____

_____

_____

What do you need to do to Totally Love Your Treasure Within?

_____

_____

_____

_____

_____

_____

What does that look like?

_____

_____

_____

_____

Reflection

Totally Lovin My Treasure Within

List 3 take aways from this chapter.

_____

_____

_____

_____

_____

_____

_____

Write a prayer that will help you Totally Love Your Treasure Within

_____

_____

_____

_____

_____

_____

_____

_____

I'M TOTALLY LOVIN MY

Totally Lovin My Boundaries

Author

Chauntina Mays

ABOUT THE AUTHOR
Chauntina Mays

Chauntina is an author, consultant, speaker, and mentor dedicated to empowering others in executive leadership and their personal lives. Currently in corporate leadership at one of the largest healthcare systems in the world, she holds an MBA in Healthcare Administration and a BS in Nursing. With over 10 years of experience in director and manager roles, Chauntina has honed her skills in effective communication, strategic planning, problem-solving, and project management. Her unwavering dedication to excellence and impactful transformation makes her a guiding force for those seeking to elevate their personal and professional journeys.

In addition to her professional work, Chauntina is a committed public servant, serving on the board of a nonprofit organization that supports domestic and sexual violence survivors. She actively advocates for social change and participates in various church and community outreach programs.

A lover of travel and literature, Chauntina enjoys exploring the world and immersing herself in both fiction and non-fiction. She is also involved in music ministry, bringing comfort and inspiration to her audiences through her vocal talents, reflecting her passion for uplifting others. Above all, Chauntina cherishes her family and her faith in the Lord.

www.talk2chauntina.com

TOTALLY LOVIN MY

Boundaries

By Chauntina Mays

It finally happened. I was worn out after a lifetime of living and spinning on the proverbial hamster wheel. I needed to feel more fulfilled. The things I had previously done with joy seemed burdensome. I was surprised and embarrassed to admit it, but I had become burnt out. I still wanted to make sure others were happy and that I had done all I could to help, but I could not find much joy. I was physically, emotionally, and sadly, even spiritually spent and all churched out. I had always been the resourceful, responsible, and ever-resilient one that others could count on, but I had hit a wall. What had happened?

I tried to think back to when I had lost myself. I sensed that, in part, the reporting of multiple deaths, including George Floyd and Breonna Taylor, was triggering. There was also the global Covid pandemic, complete with extreme social isolation and more fatalities on a more personal level. I searched even deeper within and began to see specific behavioral patterns, so I enlisted the help of a therapist.

I shared with the therapist my work and family responsibilities, church and community activities, and how I often was a resource to others. I found myself honoring a promise to be a caregiver to a friend and her elderly mother, which involved being a health advocate at the various medical facilities the friend wound up in, running between my household and theirs, and even being an ear and resource to the hired caregiver that my friend ultimately needed. The toll of bearing the crises of others with disregard for my health ultimately wore me down emotionally, financially, and physically as I found myself hypertensive, morbidly obese, and exhausted. I almost fainted one day in the hospital room of the person I was advocating for. Still, I continued to press on, holding down a full-time corporate leadership job and being a full-time MBA student.

My therapist listened patiently and quietly asked me what I did for myself. I took a breath and realized I couldn't think of one current thing I did for myself or simply because I enjoyed it. I essentially lived for the next crisis. I got up and went to work, school, and church on the weekend. Most of my true dreams and passions had taken a back seat or were past tense.

When my day ended, and I had done what my work required, and others needed, there wasn't enough time or energy left over for much else. My therapist wanted to know if I had anyone that I turned to when I needed encouragement. I admitted I had a few people but typically declined help because I didn't want to burden anyone. My therapist then rocked my world. She said, "Chauntina, you have a Savior Complex."

I was shocked and offended. I wanted to scream," You are so off track. You don't know me, Lady! I do NOT resemble that remark!". Wisely, I resisted the urge to scream, said nothing, and listened as she continued. "I think you have confused your role as a Christian. Who told you it was your job to save everyone?" she asked. "Where in the Bible did you find that Jesus saved everyone he met?"

And there it was. I didn't want to admit it, but my therapist was right. I looked back and realized that somewhere, I had connected my intrinsic value and self-worth to helping others. My value was not because I was God's child and worthy but because I was helpful and needed.

As a middle child of divorced parents, I worked to fix the broken pieces of our family and myself. I served as a peacemaker and de-escalated where I could. I would champion others but not necessarily for myself, and I carried these patterns into almost all my relationships.

My therapist's diagnosis of the savior complex brought Matthew 8:23-27 to mind. Jesus was asleep in a boat when a terrible storm suddenly arose. His disciples were terrified and awoke Jesus, begging him to save them. This story resonated with me because even amid a literal storm, I realized that Jesus saved, yet he had practiced self-care.

Christians must share the Gospel of Christ. Christians serve others but need healthy boundaries to do this work successfully. Christ had boundaries in his ministry, taking time for rest and prayer, even when teaching and healing. Christ confronted wrong behavior, was not a people pleaser, and honored his boundaries. Healthy boundaries don't wall us off or make us unavailable to others. Having healthy boundaries means we take time to recharge and recognize that we are the gatekeepers for our daily plan. We must determine our priorities. We are to help others but must also meet our personal needs and life crises. Sometimes, we can't help others, but that is okay. Jesus only helped some of the people he encountered. Our response may be yes, but sometimes our response must be a firm "no." We must be clear that our quiet "No" is a complete sentence.

Setting healthy boundaries does not mean being difficult, angry, or selfish. Healthy boundaries allow us to shine brightly for Jesus. A lack of boundaries can render us ineffective in so many areas. A candle loses its flame without its oxygen source. Likewise, we may lose our oxygen supply and burn out without boundaries.

It took me a lifetime to arrive at this place. Still, now that I am here, I am totally loving my healthy boundaries in all aspects of my life, including church. I recognize that God loves me, too, and I deserve care and love. I don't have to bear the entire weight of others' burdens, and I am comfortable allowing others to fight their own battles and in their walks of faith. Balance is essential for my well-being, and I love allowing Jesus to take the wheel!

I'm Totally Lovin My Boundaries!

Chauntina Mays

"The boundary lines have fallen for me in pleasant places; surely I have a delightful inheritance."
Psalm 16:6 (NIV)

Totally Lovin My Boundaries

Write a affirmation to help you with your boundaries?

_____

_____

_____

_____

What do you need to do to set boundaries in your life?

_____

_____

_____

_____

_____

_____

_____

_____

_____

What does that look like?

_____

_____

_____

_____

_____

 *Reflection*
Totally Lovin My Boundaries

List 3 take aways from this chapter.

_____

_____

_____

_____

_____

_____

Write a prayer that will help you Totally Love Your Boundaries

_____

_____

_____

_____

_____

_____

_____

I'M TOTALLY LOVIN MY

Totally Lovin My Ears

Author

First Lady

Esther G. Jones

ABOUT THE AUTHOR
First Lady

Esther G. Jones

I'm Lady Esther G. Jones, born August 25, 1965 in Jesup, Ga She is married to Sr. Pastor Benjamin L. Jones for 38 years. They have raised one beautiful daughter and have three grandsons. She is the First Lady of Christ Prayer Deliverance and Outreach Ministry,Inc. She is a retired educator after 30 years.

TOTALLY LOVIN MY

Ears

By First Lady Esther Grant

It all started when I was in the fourth grade and my classmates, and I were jumping the board so high which caused me to fall so hard that I busted my eardrum. During this time, my parents took me to many doctors, the only thing they were able to do was to wash it out. As I got older, I realized that I needed more support like a hearing aid. I will wear it sometimes, but it never stopped me from hearing people or hearing from God.

Romans 10:17 - So, then faith comes by hearing and hearing by the word of God. Having ears to hear is not only a natural thing but it is a spiritual thing. God has given us ears as a way of communicating one to another, I hear what you are saying, you hear what I am saying, we hear what God's saying. The more you hear, the more you know. The more you know, the more you believe. The more you believe, the more your faith builds.

John 10:27 – My sheep hear my voice, and I know them, and they know me. Isn't it a wonderful thing to be able to distinguish voices, to be able to recognize who is talking to you? To know the difference between a stranger's voice and the voices of those whom you know. Yes, yes, it is.

I thank God for forming this body with its parts, and with all the parts that make up this body, I love my ears. There are those who, though they have ears, find it difficult to hear what is being said. Sign language replaces the hearing of the ears, giving way for communication to continue.

Luke 11:28 – But He said, Blessed rather is those who hear the word of God and keep it.
Hearing the word of God is something we should want our ears to hear. Who would not want to know why they were created; what God's purpose is for them. Having ears to hear is essential. Psalm 85:8 says, I will hear what God the Lord will speak: for he will speak peace unto his people, and to his saints: but let them not turn again to folly. Just to hear the word peace brings a calmness within.

Jeremiah 33:3 – Call unto me, and I will answer thee, and shew thee great and mighty things, which thou knoweth not. Wow, having heard this with mine own ears, God wanted to show me great and mighty things. Knowing, he hears me when I call him. I am so grateful for my ears.

I love who I am, and who God made me to be. I still shy away sometimes because of hearing issues but I have learned to move forward with God's help. I am not where I should be, but I am where I need to be in God.

Philippians 4:11-13 – Not that I speak in respect of want for I have learned, in whatever state I am, therewith to be content. I know both how to be abased, and I know how to abound: everywhere and in all things, I am instructed both to be full and to be hungry, both to abound and to suffer need. I can do all things through Christ which strengtheneth me.

I have been in many situations, the issue with my hearing is but one. We must understand that in all the punches life throws at us, with Christ we are strengthened to do all things.

I was hesitant in writing this, but I thank God that He allowed me to go forward sharing with others that they may know, despite any issues they may have, be it major or minor, struggles in life will happen and there's nothing we can do to stop that. What we can do is be grateful for what we have, be thankful regardless of how it looks, hear and know who God says we are.

Ephesians 4:11-12 – It was He who appointed people for the perfecting of the saints, for the work of the ministry, for the edifying of the body of Christ. God appointed me to author my story. Never in my fifty-eight 1/2 years did I know that I would be telling my story. I know it is nobody but God. I thank God for my husband Sr. Pastor Benjamin L Jones who gave me the courage to move forward with this book when I wanted to give up. I thank God for Minister Gobbie Mazo for her input and her guidance.

Luke 6:38 says if you give, you will get. Your gift will return to you in overflowing measure, pressed down, shaken together to make room for more and running over.

Whatever measure you use to give (large or small) will be used to measure what is given back to you. I have given a part of myself to writing this, to sharing the knowledge that having issues does not determine the outcome of your life.

I totally love my ears. Even though I experienced what I did as a small child with my hearing, it has made me thankful for having ears. I hope no one will allow life's issues to cause them to not be thankful.

Totally Loving MY EARS

Esther G. Jones

Devotional

EARS

"Turning your ear to wisdom and applying your heart to understanding."

Proverbs 2:2 (NIV)

Devotional

Totally Lovin My Ears

Loving our ears involves more than just the physical ability to hear; it is about cultivating an attitude of attentiveness to wisdom, faith, and God's voice. By immersing ourselves in these scriptures and allowing their truths to resonate in our hearts, we can sharpen our listening skills, deepen our understanding, and enhance our relationship with God and others. Let us be mindful of what we choose to hear and open our ears to the life-giving messages God has for us. In doing so, we honor not only our ears but also the Creator who made them.

PRAYER

Lord, thank You for the gift of hearing, for the sounds of creation, music, and the voices of loved ones. Help me to listen with an open heart, to hear Your voice in the quiet moments, and to receive the wisdom and encouragement of those around me. May my ears be attuned to Your truth and my spirit ready to respond. In Jesus' name, Amen.

Reflection

Totally Lovin My Ears

Write a affirmation to Totally Love Ears?

_____

_____

_____

_____

How can I make space to hear God's wisdom and encouragement more clearly?

_____

_____

_____

_____

_____

_____

_____

What positive things do I hear each day, and how can I focus more on voices that lift me up and guide me?

_____

_____

_____

_____

_____

Reflection

Totally Lovin My Ears

List 3 take aways from this chapter.

_____

_____

_____

_____

_____

_____

_____

Write a prayer that will help you Totally Love Your Ears

_____

_____

_____

_____

_____

_____

_____

_____

I'M TOTALLY LOVIN MY

Totally Lovin My
Healing Process

Author
Penny Gilmore

ABOUT THE AUTHOR

Penny Gilmore

Prophet Penny Michell Gilmore is a native of Hinesville-Fort Stewart, Georgia. She is the oldest of six siblings. Prophet Gilmore took on a leadership role at a young age by assisting with raising her siblings. Penny was introduced to Jesus as a child. She sensed God's hand upon her life while attending church one Sunday morning with her grandmother. Since that day, she knew her future would consist of serving the Lord.

She is married to Reverend Cecil Gilmore and have three beautiful children: Antonio, Christopher, and Chelsea. As a firm believer in following God's timing and season; she has diligently served in ministry in various capacities. She has had the opportunity to teach people how to apply the word of God in their everyday lives. One of her favorite sayings states. "You never have to give an account of others actions but you do have to stand and give an account of how you react or respond."

Prophetess Gilmore feels strongly about maintaining consciousness of her actions as well as those in the body of Christ. Her clear gift of discernment enables her to flow in a prophetic anointing with sure authenticity. With a background as a registered nurse, Prophet Gilmore is in her junior year at the New Life Theological Seminary, located in Charlotte, North Carolina, majoring in Christian Counseling. Fueled by her passion and love for ministry, Prophet Penny Gilmore brings understanding and clarity to the workings of the Holy Spirit. She participates in preaching engagements throughout the nation. Her compassion moves her to minister to the masses and to the one.

TOTALLY LOVIN MY

Healing Process

By Penny Gilmore

Not many people will jump, shout, and say *let me suffer Lord...*

Life itself brings challenges that happen to all. Everyone that is alive can say they have experienced some pain, disappointment, heartbreak, and misfortune. We all have lost loved ones or know someone that has. Many ask the question: why do good people go through such difficulty and experience bad things?

My initial response was yes God! Why? As time progressed and my life took turns, valleys, and peaks of high points, I realized difficult times caused me to grow and endure hardness as a good soldier. My outlook on things evolved as well. I now recognize the hand of God was and is in my life through it all. I now know He specializes in the impossible. I have endured Rejection, Abandonment, Infidelity, Insecurity, Poverty, Mental anguish and attacks, Verbal, and Physical Abuse... Just to name a few...

My journey began as a kid raised by a single Mother of six children. I was the oldest of the six. This brought much responsibility. I helped raise my siblings. I had to help with meal prep, cleaning, baby-sitting, changing diapers, and preparing bottles... You name it. We were not brought up in church, but my maternal grandfather, great Aunt, and paternal grandmother would periodically take us to church, especially on Easter. I cannot remember one time that my mom attended, but she would always play gospel music and reverence God on Sunday. She made sure we knew to acknowledge him on Sunday.

God's healing hand has always been in my life. I can remember, even as a child, I would say to Him "God I am going to beat the devil up for You when I get older" I realize the enemy heard that as well. Generational Curses of poverty, fornication, and drug and alcohol addictions plagued my family line. The women were unwed and had children out of wedlock. We lived in dysfunction and did not even know it. We all lived close to each other and relied on the system for survival. I could remember using colored paper money, AKA food stamps to buy food.

One cloudy cold day my mother sent me to the store to purchase some items on a written list she prepared. I placed the book of food stamps in my pocket and began the journey to the store. I remember running, jumping, skipping, and singing all the way to the store. I placed the items on the counter and reached into my pocket to retrieve the food stamps and they were not there. My heart sank and I felt hopeless and helpless all at the same time. I began to cry and made the long trip back home empty handed.

I dreaded telling my mother that I lost the stamps and could not pay for the food. My mother began to cry and say, "Lord, what am I going to do now." I remember whispering under my breath "God help us, I am sorry I lost the money for our food, please help us." My mother was angry and sad at the same time. She bundled up her coat and back tracked and traced my steps to the store to see if she could find the stamps.

When she arrived at the store and asked the manager if anyone had turned in any food stamps, to my mother's surprise and amazement someone had found them and given them to the store's front desk. My mother was able to purchase food to feed us. One would say this was a coincidence, but I beg the differ. This was the beginning of me noticing that when I pray to God, He hears me and answers.

At the ripe age of eighteen, I decided to give my Life over to the Lord and accept salvation my first year in college. I heard a voice say, "the enemy is coming with everything he's got, but I will be with You." Instantly my mind was attacked. I began telling people that my name was LOVE. People thought I was crazy, drugged, or poisoned, there were no explanations for my behavior. I was transported to the hospital under Mental Health for an evaluation. I was prescribed multiple medications that had awful side effects. The diagnosis was mental/nervous breakdown.

My father, whom I had not seen in years, came to the college, and picked me up to take me home. I began questioning God about why He allowed this to happen to me. I felt abandoned, angry, disappointed, and betrayed. I was a Zombie because of the medications. I was hopeless again. My great Aunt took me to a revival service, and I heard a man preach deliverance. He said, "God will set you free if you believe." I pondered over those words for days. I finally got enough courage to step out on faith. I poured my medications down the toilet and headed to my bedroom. I got down on my knees and began to cry out to Jesus… I said, "Lord I came to you for salvation, but ended up with a messed-up mind… I do not want this.

I need you to heal me or get me from here Jesus. I do not want to live like this." Before I could finish my prayer, I saw and felt a big bright white warm light enter my room and touch me. I was instantly Healed and delivered. I had a sound mind and no longer had a need for medication. My family noticed the dramatic change.

One must know the signs and symptoms of a toxic relationship or situation. Recognize when you are viewed as a liability instead of an asset. If this is your case, then it is time to exit. Develop a genuine relationship with Our Heavenly Father. He loves you unconditionally. He is not like man. The Father desires the best for you and has your best interest at heart.

Totally Loving my healing process has given me the desire to be made whole and disengage myself from bitterness, regrets, resentment, insecurity, doubt, unforgiveness, poverty, fear, betrayal, and so many other bondages. God pulled me from the projects to a palace. From renting to owning. From poverty and no job depending on the system to a Registered Nurse with a bachelor's degree. What the enemy meant for bad God turned it around for my good.

Remember these Nuggets:

- Know this, if God allows it, then He has a plan and purpose for the process and a process for the purpose.
- No weapon that is formed against you will prosper. **Isaiah 54:17**
- He who hath began a good work in you will perform it until the Day of Jesus Christ. **Philippians 1:6**
- And we Know that all things work together for good to them that love God, to them who are the called according to his purpose. **Romans 8:28**

Totally Loving My Healing Process

Penny Gilmore

Devotional

TOTALLY LOVIN MY

HEALING PROCESS

And we know that all things work together for good to them that love God, to them who are the called according to his purpose.

Romans 8:28.

Devotional

Totally Lovin My Healing Process

REMEMBER THESE NUGGETS:

- If God allows it, then He has a plan and purpose for the process and for the purpose.
- No weapon that is formed against you will prosper. Isaiah 54:17
- He who hath began a good work in you will perform it until the Day of Jesus Christ Philippians 1:6
- And we know that all things work together for good to them that love God, to them who are the called according to his purpose. Romans 8:28.

PRAYER

Lord, thank You for guiding me through this healing journey. Help me to embrace each step with patience and trust in Your gentle care. May Your love bring me peace and strength as I grow closer to wholeness. In Jesus' name, Amen.

Reflection

Totally Lovin My Healing Processs

Write a affirmation for Totally Lovin My Healing Process?

_____

_____

_____

_____

What steps will you take to Totally Love Your Healing Process?

_____

_____

_____

_____

_____

_____

_____

What does that look like?

_____

_____

_____

_____

Reflection

Totally Lovin M Healing Process

List 3 take aways from this chapter.

_____

_____

_____

_____

_____

_____

_____

_____

Write a prayer that will help you Totally Love Your Healing Process

_____

_____

_____

_____

_____

_____

_____

_____

I'M TOTALLY LOVIN MY

Totally Lovin My
Travel Experience

Author

Pastor Connie Brown

ABOUT THE AUTHOR

Pastor Connie Brown

Apostle Connie Brown is the Pastor of Walking By Faith Full Gospel Ministry In 2004, the Lord intervened in my life. God placed a remarkable woman in my path who recognized potential in me that I was blind to. Despite attending church, singing in the choir, and even becoming choir president, I didn't truly know God, and I struggled with my singing ability.

In 2015, the Lord inspired me to establish Walking by Faith Ministries, where she became the pastor. From this ministry, she created the "Mother to Mother" initiative to reach out to other mothers, especially those like herself who have faced the loss of a child. Grounded in the prophetic ministry that she experienced, Pastor Connie travels extensively to fulfill the calling God has placed on my life.

Over the years, Pastor Connie has supported and officiated many weddings, as well as provided comfort and support to families during difficult times. Though she has stumbled numerous times, her trust in God's plan remains steadfast. Pastor Brown sees this as a precious opportunity to fulfill a part of my divine assignment.

TOTALLY LOVIN MY

Travel Experiences

By Pastor Connie Brown

LISTEN TOTAL *woman* **YOU** deserve this.

Remembering being a young girl I was daddy's girl. My father on a whim would jump in the car and we would be in another state. My mom did not like to travel so he would say let us go baby girl. So, my travel life begins at the age of five. Year after year we would just go. As I became a young woman, I went to work at Walmart. There was a group of women whom I knitted with, and we began a group called Traveling Angel's.

My father passed away and it broke my heart! I had lost the number one man in my life! So, I vowed to make travel my life. Let me encourage you that you can go anywhere in life that you want to. Total Woman, you must want to be free. Love yourself and live your best life. Easier said than done, you say! Well, it is, I lost my son in 2016, and I thought I was going to die. My son was murdered and decapitated after hitting a pole. At this point, I was not a total woman, but a broken woman. Yes, it took time to heal, but I decided to get up and live. I knew I wanted to see the world to push other mothers who had lost a child to encourage them to live. God gave me a vision in 2015, Walking by Faith Full Gospel Ministries, and out of that was birthed Mother to Mother.

Psalms 121:8 – says, "The LORD shall preserve thy going out and thy coming in from this time forth, and even for evermore. "What makes you a Total Woman? For me it is trusting God's plan. Have you ever been in a dark place wondering how you are going to break free? When my son died, I felt the walls of a prison. I did not want to be around anyone, did not want to bathe or go out, I just wanted to give up on life. The worst was going through emotional abuse, sexual abuse, misunderstanding, damaged by the church, and being crushed by my peers was heartbreaking.

Yes, we all have a story but even through the harshness of life, God always gets the glory from your story!

Traveling sets me free where I can go and express my feelings and my heart to others. I had the opportunity to go to Africa and Minister to hundreds of women who have lost their children.

So even across the world and another country, the pain of losing a child is truly the same. It is important for the total woman to find a place that is safe, that you feel freedom, that you feel encouraged, and that you can break free!

So, God gave me this poem and I am truly a Total Woman that is free even through the pain!

A Mother Cries When Her Son Dies

A mother cries when her son dies.

No one can understand her pain.

She dies a little with her child.

Feeling empty inside

Who can know, who can help?

Not her family, not her friend,

not the church and not even her pastor

A mother cries when her son dies.

Searching for something to fill that emptiness.

Though they try to comfort her and say it is going to be all right.

But at this time, you cannot hear, you cannot feel, and you die

inside.

You think about your other children, but feel life is over.

A mother cries when her son dies.

Wondering what you did to anger God.

Wondering why God would allow so much hurt.

So, you begin to lose yourself, faith, and all you care about

So, you blame God for the life that he gave you.

A mother cries when her son dies.

One day you hear your other children say mom what about us.

We are still here. We love and need you.

Then you begin to see your children's pain also.

And begin to realize their suffering too.

A mother cries when her son dies.

And then you hear the voice of the Lord

Daughter, I love you. Lean on me.

You are my chosen one, like me I gave my only begotten son.

I did not allow this to happen to hurt you, but to strengthen and grow you.

So, take my hand and allow me to lead you into the plan I have for you.

A mother cries when her son dies.

I allowed God to heal me.

I allowed him to lead me.

I allowed him to be the head of my life.

I allowed myself to trust him.

I allowed myself to love, laugh, and live.

One Day You Went Away

One day you went away, God saw an angel with a

broken wing. So, he decided that it was time he brought,

you are back home.

So now my earthly angel becomes My

heavenly angel. Though it hurts and the pain seems to

never go away, I know you are in God's care, and no one can love

you like the great I am.

Though I wonder why God allowed you to go, he said I also allowed

my son to die do not you know. God says I know it does not make it

easy but know that I have a plan. Do not feel sad for me because I

know we all must go one day. So, I pray for all mothers, fathers,

sons, daughters, brothers, and sisters to be strong in the Lord and

in the power of his might.

So even as the tears fall, I will lift my eyes to the heavens which

cometh my help and my help cometh from the Lord. I will always

love my son, and I will never forget the day that God brought him

into my life.

I know that God has a place for you in heaven so

I am strong now; I am even better now. I am thanking God for the three precious children that I still have.

So, to my precious son in heaven know that we love you and miss you and we are going to take care of one another because we know this is your desire.

So blessed to have had you as my son. I love you so much.

Proverbs 3:23 says," Then shalt thou walk in thy way safely, and thy foot shall not stumble."

These poems help me be that total woman. So, as I travel, I can author my story and all my experiences. Begin to journal your journey! Total woman you would enjoy a lifestyle of traveling. There are many beautiful people to encounter and share the goodness of God with. This is a wonderful way to minister and to network with great people.

Total woman, you are phenomenal. God has graced you to do anything that your heart desires. Travel the world and begin to see the different things that God has to offer. He loves you so much. Whom the son has set free is free indeed. May your travels bring you blessings, friendships, relationships, and love because you are a Total Woman!

Totally Lovin MY TRAVEL EXPERIENCES

Pastor Connie Brown

"I know that there is nothing better for people than to be happy and to do good while they live. That each of them may eat and drink and find satisfaction in all their toil—this is the gift of God."

Ecclesiastes 3:12-13 (NIV)

Totally Lovin My Travel Experiences

Write a affirmation regarding your Travel Experiences?

_____

_____

_____

_____

Write about your current and future Travel experiences?

_____

_____

_____

_____

_____

_____

_____

_____

What does that look like?

_____

_____

_____

_____

Reflection

Totally Lovin My Travel Experinces

List 3 take aways from this chapter.

_____

_____

_____

_____

_____

_____

_____

Write a prayer that will help you Totally Love Your Travel Experiences

_____

_____

_____

_____

_____

_____

_____

_____

I'M TOTALLY LOVIN MY

Totally Lovin
My Start Over

Author

Dr. Misty Beards

ABOUT THE AUTHOR

Dr. Misty Beards

Dr. Misty Beards is a native of South Carolina. She is a mother of three and a grandmother of three. Dr. Beards loves the Lord and loves to serve God's people with her talents and gifts. She is a 5x author and Master Life Coach. She is the CEO of New Discovery Life Coaching Institute, CEO of Totally Lovin Me Magazine and Publishing Company, and the Founder of "The Healing Kitchen" and Founder of "Heal-Her Retreats. Dr. Misty never meets strangers and always loves sharing the love of Jesus with all.

Dr. Misty Beards has served at His Kingdom Ministries in Durham, North Carolina for over 10 years. Her amazing leaders and spiritual parents are Apostle Janice and Bishop Randall Thomas

www.tlmmpublishing.com

www.drmistybeards.com

www.totallylovinme.com

TOTALLY LOVIN MY

Start-Over

By Dr. Misty Beards

" I have always been the kind of woman; if I am with you, I am with you. I have always been afraid of rejection and break-ups. It is that place of having to start over. Who wants to start over? I realize that the fear of starting over causes us to compromise and overlook the red flags in all relationships. Therefore, we stay in situations longer than necessary and accrue unnecessary hurt and pain.

I have been discovering that starting over has its advantages. When we take time to heal our insecurities and inadequacy, we can see the web in which we have been entangled. You begin to see the cycles and behaviors that you have been tolerating. You can see where boundaries have not been set.

When you have opportunities to start over, embrace them. Look into yourself and find the excitement of recreating what you desire, not what you settled for or handed to you. I realize that my worthiness is one that I must accept and embrace for myself. No one can tell you of your value and worth. As a woman, you were created by the hand of God. This automatically makes you worthy of the Father's goodness for you.

I understand that our lives have not been easy. Life has thrown us many curve balls, and most of the time, we have felt like we just needed to take what was handed to us. Well, great woman, let me tell you that we no longer have to accept the status quo. You are powerful, and you are a speaking spirit. You were given the authority to speak about something, and it happened.

No matter what situation you are in at this moment, you can start over. Look at the canvas of your life today. Does it look like what you imagined? Have you allowed other people 'to paint their image of you? And you patterned yourself after that? If so, do not beat yourself up. Just start over. Make new decisions about your day! You are in control of what you will and will not accept now. It does not have to be an argument, being angry, or done wrong to start over. It only requires one to look in the mirror and realize that this part or that part needs to change.

Although it took several circumstances to make me look around, I praise God for those circumstances. I have become an embrace of startovers. Now, I understand that it does not mean that I stay in a cycle of constantly starting over, but I pay attention to my mistakes or what God reveals, and I make a new change. I cultivate that change and allow myself to evolve in my new change.

Let me empower you, love yourself enough, and give yourself the grace to start over. You do not owe anyone an exclamation as to why you are changing. You walk out of the change, no matter what the opposition. I totally love my start-over. This is my opportunity to see through the eyes of God for my life. It allows time for me to gain new ground and discover the hidden treasure within me. It allows me to display a more excellent standard of self-respect and self-honor. I have gained momentum as I discover that I can do all things through Christ that strengthens me.

As we start over, we are walking a new path. This path, of course, does not look like what we are used to. People, places, and things will fall off, making your circle small. You can expect this. God places a new attraction on us as we evolve in our new lives. Now, we surround ourselves with people who genuinely celebrate us, hanging in with us in our vulnerable times. I call them your **"TRIBE."**

Freedom to be yourself is a fantastic feeling. I would not trade it for anything in the world. It took me a long time to get here. My life was soaked in marriage, children, ministry, starting a business, and trying to make it. When I said that, I was not all around happy. I lost myself somewhere and could not find myself. It came with some pain when the opportunity came, but I understood that this was my chance to love Misty without caring what others thought or felt. God is so gracious, loving, and kind. There is a total woman within that awaits to arise.

A woman is longing for a moment's decision to start over. She is within you. Her purpose, style, laughter, enjoyment of life, and positive connections are within you. Allow no one to conceal you in a box. God frees us, so therefore be free. You deserve greatness. You are free to allow life to be good to you. You can demand others to treat you great and be kind to you.

When we arise, we permit others to do the same. It begins with a start-over. Your life is going to shine so brightly. You have been waiting for this. Now, take out a new canvas and ensure it is large enough to hold everything you can imagine. Put no limitations on your imagination and goals for yourself. Dream big, then dream bigger, and now execute! You will be amazed at what you will now become. It has been there from the day of your creation. **Are you ready?**

Totally Lovin My Start Over

Dr. Misty Beards

"See, I am doing a new thing! Now it springs up; do you not perceive it? I am making a way in the wilderness and streams in the wasteland."

Isaiah 43:19 (NIV)

Reflection

Totally Lovin My Start Over

Write a affirmation for Totally Lovin My Start Over

_____

_____

_____

_____

What steps will you take to Totally Love Your Start Over?

_____

_____

_____

_____

_____

_____

_____

_____

What does that look like?

_____

_____

_____

_____

Reflection

Totally Lovin My Start Over

List 3 take aways from this chapter.

_____

_____

_____

_____

_____

_____

_____

Write a prayer about Totally Lovin My Start Over

_____

_____

_____

_____

_____

_____

_____

_____

I'M TOTALLY LOVIN MY

Totally Lovin My Determination

Author

Kimberly Blount

ABOUT THE AUTHOR

Kimberly Blount

My name is Kimberly ; I am the founder of Freeing To Be Fit LLC. The concept for my business is that you are only as fit as your entire being. the mind body and soul. I received my bachelor's degree in Sports and Health Sciences with a minor in Exercise Sciences in 2016.

I am currently certified as a Personal trainer, Group fitness instructor, Sport nutritionist, Lifestyle weight management specialist and Behavior change specialist. I am a three-time author of the book trilogy Blue Girls Turned Gold. Lastly but not least I am the proud mother of three and grandmother of one. I am thankful to have this opportunity to encourage other in this book Total Woman Within Anthology.

TOTALLY LOVIN MY

Determination

By Kimberly Blount

"**D**etermination is a firm sensation of purpose and commitment to reaching goals or following a particular path regardless of the challenges you might experience. The personality traits of a determined individual are:

1. **Faithfulness**
2. **Consistency**
3. **Gratitude**
4. .**Authenticity**
5. **No fear of failure**
6. **Big dreamer**
7. **Decisiveness**
8. **Resiliency**
9. **Discipline**
10. **Hardworking**

Always remember life is something that you make happen or you let happen to you.

Working Towards a Better Tomorrow

In 2006, I was a 21-year-old newlywed with a two-year-old with my whole life in front of me. Within the life of my marriage, I received my Associate in Arts (AA) degree, Bachelor of Science (BS) degree and had two more children. Since my husband was in the military, I thought it made sense for me to be a stay-at-home mother. After almost twelve years of marriage, ours appeared to be ending. Once I realized that there was a real possibility that this would happen, I tried everything I could to save it. It was too late.

In the efforts to save my marriage I found a part time job. Since I had not worked in almost seven years it was hard for me to find employment in my field of study. In June of 2018 after working at a part time job for about a year barely making enough to make ends meet God blessed me with a full-time position with a local hospital.

In November of 2018, my divorce was finalized, and it was one of the lowest points of my life. I was living in a military town with virtually no one to assist me with my needs. I felt alone with no help! My youngest was only a toddler at that time. It was hard to find a reasonably priced daycare that had exceptional ratings. The daycare he was previously in I could not afford. Thankfully, I was able to find a home daycare that worked with me. My oldest at this time was problematic and was giving me hell.

My poor middle baby was lost in the mix, and I was barely holding it together. The Lord knew I was at wits end and felt depleted. I did not want to move back home, and I refused to give my ex-husband the satisfaction of seeing me fail.

Single parenthood is not for the weak. One thing I knew was I had to make my situation work. I was working long hours and barely saw my children. I honestly believe that when it is time to move from a situation (job) you must decide what is best for your family. Working twelve-hour shifts and every other weekend, not spending quality time with my children became unbearable. I could not continue this way, caring for my children and taking care of my personal mental health at the same time was a challenge. Something had to change.

I worked at the hospital for two years. In 2020 I decided I needed something more accommodating to my life circumstances. One thing is for sure, once I make up my mind to do something GOD does the rest. Within a few weeks of looking for a new job with better hours and more pay I was offered a position with a clinic in Hinesville, Georgia. I started employment in August of 2022. My hours were Monday- Friday and occasionally on Saturday. Things were looking up; the job was decent, and I had the opportunity to work within the community.

But I had higher hopes, and in 2022, after about a year and a half on the job at the clinic, I realized it no longer served me, and my life changed. Here comes another life change. My son had weekly appointments for speech therapy, and I could not take the time off that was needed for him to make his appointments. The job itself became stressful due to new management. After whirlwind after whirlwind, I started to look for another job. I never gave up!

In April of 2022, I found a job working at another clinic. It was farther away, and the pay was less. It was a minor setback financially that turned out to be a great blessing in the end. While working at that job, I never stopped looking and talking about determination.

In August 2022, the search ended. Today I am thankful to work for the Federal Government. By the grace of God, I am here. I have my own benefits and a retirement plan. Working for the Federal Government has opened other doors of opportunity for advancement.

Since my divorce I have been determined to have a career and success that gives stability to my family. My goal has always been to ensure my children's needs are met and they are healthy well-rounded individuals. This journey and the road to career success have been taxing. There were many times I wanted to give up and throw in the towel. But I persevered. Through this process, I gained wisdom, knowledge, and experience as I elevated and succeeded on this journey called life. I was Determined to Win through Consistency!

Isaiah (ESV) 57:10 You were wearied with the length of your way, but you did not say "It is hopeless," you found new life for your strength, and so you were not faint.

Freeing to be fit

Totally Lovin MY DETERMINATION

Kimberly Blount

"May the God who gives endurance and encouragement give you the same attitude of mind toward each other that Christ Jesus had, so that with one mind and one voice you may glorify the God and Father of our Lord Jesus Christ."

Romans 15:5-6 (NIV)

Reflection

Totally Lovin My Determination

Write a affirmation for Totally Lovin My Determination

_____
_____
_____

What steps will you take to Totally Love Your Determination ?

_____
_____
_____
_____
_____
_____
_____

What does that look like?

_____
_____
_____
_____

Reflection

Totally Lovin My Start Over

List 3 take aways from this chapter.

_____

_____

_____

_____

_____

_____

_____

_____

Write a prayer about Totally Lovin My Determination

_____

_____

_____

_____

_____

_____

_____

_____

_____

I'M TOTALLY LOVIN MY

Totally Lovin My Sisterhood

Author

Elaina Diggs

ABOUT THE AUTHOR

Elaina Diggs

I am an Obstetrics and Gynecology Nurse Practitioner. On my days off, I am an author writing stories for the hopeless romantics. It has been truly an honor being part if this Anthology to support women. My story of Totally Lovin My Sisterhood encourages women to surround yourself with a sisterhood that will pray you through the battles and praise with you when those battles are won.

TOTALLY LOVIN MY

Sisterhood

By Elania Diggs

" **M**any people have lived by the quote, "if you can count your true friends on one hand, then you are truly a lucky person." Because of this so-called luck of having five true friends, this same group of people believe that these five friends will never leave you nor forsake you. How is that working out for you? Whomever coined that phrase must not have had very much faith, hope, joy, or love. This type of luck sounds very lonely to me. Well, when you are ready to stop being the lucky one, I will tell you all about being the Blessed one. Go ahead. I will be here. I have nothing but time because I am already Blessed. For you to truly understand, I need to start at the beginning. Are you ready?

It took a while for me to follow the tracks of my tears to truly understand the life I had been living. The journey backwards was harder for me than when I was living it in real time. The hardest part is you must open your heart and mind to some painful, ugly truth while all along owning your part in all of it. Sure, it is very easy to blame others. It is a comfort measure and a shortcut to compensate for an unpleasant or unwelcome situation, but there is no healing in easy. What I learned on this journey to healing is that I was living life in waves, up and down, head-first, never on my feet, and on my own accord. I have named it 'The Bungee Jumper.'

In my early childhood, I was a happy little girl. I grew up in a large Christian family with church a few times a week, on a regular basis. Whether it be church all-day Sunday, ending with dinner in the reception hall or choir rehearsals. I only had one younger sister, but our family was quite extended with grandparents, aunties, uncles, and lots of cousins. Even today I am not one hundred percent sure which cousin belongs to which auntie or uncle, that is how close we all were. It honestly did not matter because we belonged to each other. We were also a family of singers. I followed in the footsteps of my mother and aunties by singing in the choir since I was five years old. This was yet another extension of family for me, the church, and the choir. This is where my love for Jesus began and was nurtured. My first true friend. This was all I would ever need, right?

By the time I was ten years old, my parents had divorced, and my mother had remarried. This sparked the exile and disappearance of my daddy due to this new family. With this new marriage, came two additional older siblings and a new baby coming. So, this union placed me right in the middle. Studies show that the middle child often feels the need to compete for parental attention against both the older and younger siblings.

So, it begins. This fight for attention was a fight for love and belonging which stems from feelings of abandonment.

I was never truly abandoned but having to share my family with "outsiders" was the source of my pain. Of the large number of people who had been "inside" my life all these years, I never felt the pain of anger and possession until hearing someone else calling my mother mommy.

Over the next few years, a loud voice inside overwhelmed me with unpleasant feelings, thoughts, emotions, and beliefs. This is where the entanglement of a long cord of unfulfilled voids, bound at my feet, was developed. This is the point at which I began the climb of running from my pain, from those who love me, and from Jesus. Now graduating from high school, my search to fill these voids had taken me to new heights. Standing on the ledge of young adulthood, expecting the thrill of a lifetime, I took the plunge. Falling head-first, in and out of relationships, sex, alcohol, children out of wedlock, and landing face first into abuse.

Really? How did I end up here? Where did the thrill of a lifetime go? The longer my life hung in the balance of abuse, the more broken I became, until eventually I was completely shattered. Among those pieces were homelessness, hopelessness, loneliness, fear, anxiety, depression, sadness, and more. I felt worthless and unloved. Honestly, I was not sure that for which was left to live. However, the one thing I never lost was faith. It was always with me. It just needed to be awakened again. Remember my first friend? The Bible says in **Deuteronomy 31: 8** "The Lord himself goes before you and will be with you; He will never leave you nor forsake you. Do not be afraid; do not be discouraged." He was always there. In my son's strength and in my daughter's joy.

There are more pieces to this story, but I will tell you this. Right after that realization of His presence still in my life, I was invited to church. One invite after another, I began to sing again, which led me to my friend again. That long elastic bungee cord of unfulfilled voids was cut by God's grace, forcing me to Stand. Now I Stand on His word, on His love, and on His sisterhood for which He has fulfilled my every void.

Why a sisterhood you ask? Because God did not plan for us to go through life alone. "For where two or three gather in my name, there am I with them" **(Matthew 18:20).**

I see Him everywhere now. In the sister whose shy and tender heart is always willing to be brave and stand for her sisters. In the sister who was faced with a great challenge at the birth of her son, whose faith has taught me that there is nothing that God cannot do. The sister who has faced single parenthood of three girls alone, wears the crown of motherhood with grace, strength, and unconditional love. In the sister who prays with so much power and strength that chains are broken with the sound of her voice. In the sister who is the glue who holds the many parts of her family together despite the things that chip away at the cracks on the outside.

In the sister who is friend to everyone and foe to none, who has taught me that whether it is your home or your heart that you welcome all, they are both the same safe place. In the sister who is the mother that leads her flock with the voice of an angel, telling the love stories of God. And so many more.

I realized that all those broken pieces are a part of me and who I am. God never promised that life would be perfect, but He gave us the armor to fight those battles while leaving the war to Him. It has been said that "life is not about the quantity of friends you have. It is about the quality of friends you have." I am totally Lovin' my sisterhood who surrounds me when the battle begins and celebrates with me when the war is won. I pray that you seek and find the sisters that surround you with God's blessings. **I am Not lucky. I am Blessed.**

Totally Lovin My Sisterhood

Elaina Diggs

Devotional

TOTALLY LOVIN MY

SISTERHOOD

So humble yourselves under the mighty power of God, and at the right time He will lift you up in honor. Give all your worries and cares to God, for He cares about you.

1 Peter 5:6-7 (NLT)

Devotional

Totally My Sisterhood

STOP!! Now Play this song: "I Surrender All" by CeCe Winans.

Once you have surrendered it all to Jesus, you may be left feeling completely broken. And that is ok. Sometimes we need to experience a little brokenness to remind us that when we lay all our broken pieces at His feet, He puts us back together with Grace. While playing this song: "Gracefully Broken" by Tasha Cobbs Leonard, close your eyes, lift your hands to Heaven and present those broken pieces to Him. Allow God to make you whole again.

PRAYER

Heavenly Father,

I thank You for the gift of sisterhood and the bonds that connect us. Help me to love and support my sisters with grace, understanding, and compassion. May we lift each other up, encourage one another, and grow together in Your love. Bless our relationships so they reflect Your heart. In Jesus' name, Amen.

Elainia Diggs

Reflection

Totally My Sisterhood

Write a affirmation for Totally Lovin Your Sisterhood?

_____

_____

_____

What steps will you take to Totally Love your sisterhood connections?

_____

_____

_____

_____

_____

_____

What does that look like?

_____

_____

_____

_____

Reflection

Totally My Sisterhood

List 3 take aways from this chapter.

_____

_____

_____

_____

_____

_____

_____

Write a prayer that will help you Totally Love Your Sisterhood

_____

_____

_____

_____

_____

_____

_____

_____

I'M TOTALLY LOVIN MY

Totally Lovin
My Luxe Life

Author

Daniela-Gabrielle Smallwood

ABOUT THE AUTHOR

Daniela-Gabrielle Smallwood

Daniela-Gabrielle Smallwood , is a bestselling author of eighteen business & professional development books, a sought-out motivational speaker, and dynamic marketing correspondent .

As an entrepreneur, intrapreneur, and Head of Marketing and Communications for one of the largest black owned hospitality companies in the U.S., Daniela-Gabrielle has embraced her purpose-driven assignment to empower and equip high-performing leaders through education, business, and entertainment.

Faith Lane Corporation, Founder & CEO
4301 50th Street NW Suite 300 PMB 1018
Washington, DC 20016

www.faithlanesociety.com
www.inthefaithlane.com

TOTALLY LOVIN MY

Luxe Life

By Daniela Gabrielle-Smallwood

"I never understood why we have to wait until a special occasion to use the good China. As a kid, I always questioned why every day was not approached or seen as special. Why did we reserve great experiences for a few times a year? I wanted every day to feel special."

Every day is extraordinary, the ability to fill all the days of my life with minute details that made my life feel beautiful. This sentiment was the foundation and echoed in my mind as I embarked on my journey towards embracing a luxe life. A life where every moment, no matter how ordinary, became infused with elegance, beauty, and intentionality. It began with a simple act - drinking out of fancy wine glasses. From there, it blossomed into a celebration of self, an affirmation of my worth, and a declaration of the abundant life I was meant to live.

A Celebration of Self

Cultivating a culture of celebration begins within, with a profound celebration of self. But what does it mean to celebrate oneself? It is about acknowledging and honoring the unique qualities, talents, and beauty that make us who we are. It is about embracing our worthiness and giving ourselves permission to bask in the light of our own greatness.

Scripture is replete with verses that support the concept of celebration. In Psalm 139:14, we are reminded that we are fearfully and wonderfully made, and in Ephesians 2:10, we are described as God's masterpiece, created for good works. These passages affirm the inherent value and worthiness that each of us possesses simply by virtue of being created in the image of God.

Giving ourselves permission to celebrate ourselves is not an act of selfishness, but rather an act of self-love and empowerment. It is recognizing that we cannot pour from an empty cup and that by nurturing ourselves, we are better equipped to serve and uplift others.

When we are connected to the greatness that God sees in us, we can pour so much more into the world around us.

Breaking free from the mindset that says the celebration of self is selfish is essential for personal growth and fulfillment. It is about understanding that self-care and self-love are not indulgences, but necessities for living a balanced and purposeful life. When we prioritize our own well-being, we become more resilient, compassionate, and effective in our relationships and endeavors.

Celebrating ourselves also has far-reaching benefits beyond our individual lives. It sets an example for others to follow, inspiring them to embrace their own worthiness and greatness. It creates a ripple effect of positivity and empowerment, breaking toxic cultures that contend with the culture of celebration and replacing them with environments where all are encouraged to shine.

An Affirmation of Worth

Living a luxe life is not just about material indulgence; it is about cultivating an Affirmation of Worth that transcends the external trappings of wealth and luxury. Affirmation, in this context, refers to the conscious recognition and acceptance of one's inherent value and significance. Worth, on the other hand, speaks to the intrinsic dignity and importance that everyone possesses simply by virtue of being created in the image of God.

Biblical proof of our worth in God abounds throughout scripture. In Psalm 139:14, we are reminded that we are fearfully and wonderfully made, intricately woven together by the hands of the Creator. Ephesians 2:10 declares that we are God's masterpiece, created for good works that He prepared in advance for us to do. These verses affirm that our worth is not based on our external circumstances or achievements, but on our identity as beloved children of God.

Biblical proof of our worth in God abounds throughout scripture. In Psalm 139:14, we are reminded that we are fearfully and wonderfully made, intricately woven together by the hands of the Creator. Ephesians 2:10 declares that we are God's masterpiece, created for good works that He prepared in advance for us to do. These verses affirm that our worth is not based on our external circumstances or achievements, but on our identity as beloved children of God.

Living a luxe life as an Affirmation of Worth means embracing who we are in Christ and allowing that truth to permeate every aspect of our being. It means recognizing that our worthiness is not contingent on external validation or material possessions, but on our relationship with the One who created us. This inner transformation is the foundation upon which the outer trappings of luxury living are built.

The jewelry, travel, and material comforts that often accompany a luxe lifestyle are not the primary focus; rather, they reflect the inner abundance that comes from knowing our worth in God. When we embrace our worthiness, we gain the confidence to walk boldly in faith towards the assignments of greatness that God has prepared for us. We become beacons of light, radiating the love and grace of Christ to those around us.

You cannot unlock the grandeur of God without embracing the worthiness that comes from Him. When we accept that we are worthy to be a big deal and walk in big deal seasons, we enter multi dimensions of luxe living that transcend the temporal and usher in the eternal. So let us affirm our worth in God, embrace the abundant life that He has promised us, and step boldly into the destiny of greatness that He has prepared for each one of us.

A Declaration of Abundant Life

Leading a luxe life is a declaration of abundance, a bold affirmation of God's will for us as believers. Abundance, in the biblical sense, is not just about material wealth, but encompasses every area of our lives - spiritually, emotionally, physically, and financially. It is God's desire for us to live in abundance, to experience His goodness and provision in every aspect of our being.

Scripture is clear about God's will for abundance in the lives of His children. In John 10:10, Jesus declares, "I have come that they may have life, and have it to the full." This abundant life that Jesus promises is not just a future hope; it is a present reality for those who believe. **Psalm 23:5** speaks of God's overflowing provision, saying, "My cup overflows." And in **Philippians 4:19**, we are assured that God will supply all our needs according to His riches in glory in Christ Jesus.

Every act of luxury, whether it is treating ourselves to a lavish vacation, investing in high-quality products, or surrounding ourselves with beauty and elegance, is a tangible expression of our faith in God's abundance.

Spiritually, leading a luxe life activates our access to wealth and abundance by aligning our hearts and minds with God's promises. When we believe that we are worthy of abundance and embrace the blessings that God has in store for us, we open ourselves up to receive His abundance in ever-increasing measure. This spiritual activation creates a fertile ground for multiplication, as God's blessings flow freely into our lives and overflow to bless others.

The scripture that says, "declare a thing and it shall be established" **(Job 22:28)** speaks to the power of our words and beliefs to shape our reality. When we declare abundance over our lives and live in alignment with that declaration, we create a powerful atmosphere of faith and expectation. Every act of luxury becomes a declaration of faith, establishing a life of abundance that reflects God's goodness and provision.

Leading a luxe life is not just about indulgence; it is about living in alignment with God's will for abundance and allowing His blessings to flow freely into every area of our lives. So let us declare abundance over ourselves and step boldly into the lavish, extravagant life that God has prepared for us.

Totally Loving My Luxe Life

Daniela-Gabrielle Smallwood

Devotional

TOTALLY LOVIN MY

LUXE LIFE

"Do not conform to the pattern of this world, but be transformed by the renewing of your mind. Then you will be able to test and approve what God's will is—his good, pleasing and perfect will."

Romans 12:2 (NIV)

Devotional

Totally Lovin My Luxe LIfe

May I walk in the light of your love, connected to the greatness that you see in me, and may I shine brightly, illuminating the path for others to follow. Guide me in cultivating a culture of celebration within myself and in the world around me, that all may know the joy and freedom that comes from embracing our true selves.

PRAYER

Heavenly Father,

I come to You with gratitude for the blessings of this life. Help me to embrace the beauty of my unique journey and to walk boldly in the light of Your love. May I be continually reminded of the greatness You have placed within me, shining as a beacon for those around me. Guide me to cultivate a spirit of celebration within myself and to spread joy in my daily walk. May my life reflect the freedom and joy that come from living authentically in You. Let my heart overflow with gratitude, and may I bring warmth, love, and encouragement to all I encounter. In Your love, I stand, grateful and empowered. Amen.

Daniela-Gabrielle Smallwood

Reflection

Totally Lovin My Luxe Life

Write a affirmation for Totally Lovin Your Luxe Life?

_____

_____

_____

_____

What steps will you take to Totally Love Your Luxe Life?

_____

_____

_____

_____

_____

_____

_____

What does that look like?

_____

_____

_____

_____

Reflection

Totally Lovin My Luxe Life

List 3 take aways from this chapter.

_____

_____

_____

_____

_____

_____

_____

Write a prayer that will help you Totally Love Your Luxe Life

_____

_____

_____

_____

_____

_____

_____

_____

I'M TOTALLY LOVIN MY

Totally Lovin My Body

Author

Kayla Newman

ABOUT THE AUTHOR

Kayla Newman

Pastor Kayla Newman is one of the Executive Pastor at His Kingdom Ministries located in Durham, NC where she has served in the ministry for 17 years.

Under the leadership of Apostle Janice Thomas, Bishop Randall Thomas, and the leading of the Holy Spirit, she has been on a fast track for God. Pastor Kayla, daughter of Deacon James and Edna Newman grew up in Clinton, NC. She attended North Carolina Central University where she received her B.A in Political Science and minor in English in 2004.

Later in 2012, Pastor Kayla received an Associate Degree in Biblical Studies from His Kingdom Ministries Covenant Bible College. Making Durham her home, she has pursued vast careers but has found her gift as a serial entrepreneur. She is the owner and operator of KJslay.com and Bodied by KJ. Pastor Kayla Newman is sold out for the Lord and is truly walking by faith and not by sight.

IG: @kaylajames_ cc
TikTok: @kaylajames_cc
FB: Kayla Newman

TOTALLY LOVIN MY

Body

The Body Made For Me

By Kayla Newman

Beloved, I wish above all things that thou mayest prosper and be in HEALTH, even as thy soul prospers. (3rd John 2)

"I don't like my hips!" "I don't have a butt." "I hate my arms!" "I'm sick of looking at my gut, and I can't fit anything." STOP IT! Why are you talking to yourself that way? Why are you tearing down God's beautiful creation? How can you totally love yourself if you are constantly pointing out your imperfections? Everything is beautiful about you, and I do mean EVERYTHING! Life is constantly happening on a regular basis, and it will cause major changes in your body as you age, but that does not mean you have to accept it. It is time to make a change. It is time to change your perspective about how you see your body.

First, let us take inventory of how you are treating your body. Your temple must be taken care of from the inside out. Have you ever heard of the phrase "*Eat to Live,* Not *Live to Eat*"? Well, a lot of us are living to eat. Food, for many, is a crutch of comfort. We eat to celebrate achievements. We eat when we are sad and depressed. We eat when we are bored. We just **EAT**! GOD, help me control what I put in my belly because I enjoy food! God help me to be mindful of what I put in my body. I cannot eat junk and expect my body to respond in the healthiest way possible.

God has put everything here on earth to make sure that your body has everything it needs. Hey girl, are you drinking your water? Do you eat green, leafy vegetables? Or do you fill your gut with sweets, fatty foods, and things that break the body down? When you are totally loving you, that means you do the challenging thing and **CHECK YOUR PLATE**.

Sis, are you moving your body? Research has found that doing some type of physical activity at least once or twice a week can help lower your chances of heart disease or stroke. You were created to move. So, let us get up off the couch, get out of the chair, and MOVE. And while some of you will completely scoff at the idea of going to the gym or exercising, it is the physical activity that will keep you feeling better, younger, and more energized! When you are totally loving your body, you embrace your imperfections, but you also embrace the need to be better. Maybe you do not want to go to the gym, well, walk around your neighborhood. Maybe you like to dance. Maybe you like to play a sport. Or maybe ride a bike. Whatever it is, you **MUST** move your body.

What is your mental impression about your body? Or, in other words, what is your perception of the body HE made? How you think about yourself will manifest naturally. You must be willing to capture those thoughts and change how you view yourself. **2 Corinthians 10:5** says, "*casting down imaginations,* and every high thing that exalteth itself against the knowledge of God and bringing into captivity every thought to the obedience of Christ." In other words, you should pull down all the negative thoughts about your body and think about those things that will cause your body to flourish.

It is easy to talk about what you do not like about yourself, but are you doing anything to change it? You cannot want a solution to the problem but decide to destroy yourself with your own words because you struggle with the process. Now do not get me wrong, no one is saying become delusional about the condition that your body is in. But what I am saying is that projecting negative thoughts will produce negative results. Projecting positive thoughts will produce positive results.

Hey lady, **YOU ARE NOT ALONE!** We all have struggled when it comes to our body. I cannot begin to tell you how many times I have gone back and forth with exercise, nutrition, and how I feel about my body. Now do not get me wrong, fitness and nutrition have always been a part of my life, but I lacked constant consistency. There would be moments that I was doing great and then life would happen, and I would have to start all over again. I am what you would classify as an emotional eater. If things went left in my life, I would turn to food for comfort. I would turn to all the things that were not good for me and use them to ease the pain instead of turning to Jesus. And sis, I might have been praying, but I was stuffing my face at the same time.

It is easy to talk about what you do not like about yourself, but are you doing anything to change it? You cannot want a solution to the problem but decide to destroy yourself with your own words because you struggle with the process. Now do not get me wrong, no one is saying become delusional about the condition that your body is in. But what I am saying is that projecting negative thoughts will produce negative results. Projecting positive thoughts will produce positive results.

Hey lady, **YOU ARE NOT ALONE!** We all have struggled when it comes to our body. I cannot begin to tell you how many times I have gone back and forth with exercise, nutrition, and how I feel about my body. Now do not get me wrong, fitness and nutrition have always been a part of my life, but I lacked constant consistency. There would be moments that I was doing great and then life would happen, and I would have to start all over again. I am what you would classify as an emotional eater. If things went left in my life, I would turn to food for comfort. I would turn to all the things that were not good for me and use them to ease the pain instead of turning to Jesus. And sis, I might have been praying, but I was stuffing my face at the same time.

In 2020, I reached my heaviest weight, and it was at that point that I decided that I could no longer live this way. So, I prayed and asked God to help me produce a way to balance what I am eating and to stay active. I stopped wanting to fit into a certain aesthetic or look like a certain body type. I embraced my body and said how can I make this body better. I let go of the fad diets. I stopped thinking I could lose twenty pounds in 5 days and realized that slow and steady wins the race. This does not mean I get it right all the time, but I do not quit. God has graced me with discipline to watch my plate and move my body. He can do the same for you. Keep going!

"*I am beautiful!*" "I am fearfully, and wonderfully made." "*I am strong.*" "I can move, and I am flexible!" "I love my body, and I want to take care of ME." "I will love myself from the inside out." "*I AM TOTALLY LOVING ME; THE BODY HE MADE.*

Totally Lovin THE BODY HE MADE

Pastor Kayla Newman

187

"I praise you because I am fearfully and wonderfully made; your works are wonderful, I know that full well."

Psalm 139:14

Reflection

Totally Lovin My Body

Write a affirmation for Totally Lovin My Body

_____
_____
_____
_____

What steps will you take to Totally Love Your Body?

_____
_____
_____
_____
_____
_____
_____

What does that look like?

_____
_____
_____
_____

Reflection
Totally Lovin My Body

List 3 take aways from this chapter.

_____

_____

_____

_____

_____

_____

Write a prayer about Totally Lovin My Body

_____

_____

_____

_____

_____

_____

_____

I'M TOTALLY LOVIN MY

Totally Lovin My Story

Author

Takia Lovette

ABOUT THE AUTHOR

Takia Lovette

Takia Lovett is an ordained minister, mentor, life coach and author. She founded LUV (Ladies Uniquely Virtuous) Ministries where she hosts the annual Makidada Weekend Retreat, LADY (Loving and Developing Yourself) Circle, a mentor program for girls ages 13-18 and a virtual platform known as "Liberation Room," for women working to build generational legacy over generational strongholds. Takia lives confidently in the uniqueness of who God created her to be, and through coaching on healing the "neurospirit," she works with others to do the same.

TOTALLY LOVIN MY

Story

By Takia Lovett

God Writes the Best Stories

"... I will proclaim your goodness, yours alone. You have taught me ever since I was young, and I still tell of your wonderful acts." - **Psalms 71:16-17**

My life is a divinely composed mixtape ghostwritten by God, Langston Hughes, Edgar Albert Guest, Zora Neale Hurston, and Maya Angelou. I can easily quote from their writings as a description. Understand, *"life for me hasn't been no crystal stair."* I did not grow up in the projects, nor was I dumpster diving for food, yet the power and significance of the poem *"Don't Quit"* is encrypted in my DNA. Zora did not know it, but my eyes, too, *"Were Watching God,"* as I eventually learned, *"I'm a woman phenomenally, phenomenal woman that's me."*

Indignity: The Story of My Beginning

There is not a period in my life where I do not recall being ashamed of some aspect of my life. My mother had a drug addiction and suffered from undiagnosed, and therefore untreated, mental illness. She ping-ponged between going to church and going to the streets. My daddy had an inconsistent presence in our lives. She remarried a pedophile and physically abusive man; add abandonment, additional mother wounds, and sexual abuse traumas experienced at the hands of the other family members to this fragile foundation, and I enter puberty with my self-esteem in a deficit.

The bullying and indignity I endured allowed me to downplay everything about myself. I would do almost anything to fit in. I lied about inconsequential things. I stole to have what my "friends" had. I started having sex, including experimenting with girls, at the age of twelve and became a mother at 15. As a high school senior, I was a teen mother of five, though I had only given birth to one child.

I lived in a two-bedroom apartment with my son, youngest sister, brother, nephew, and niece. My "parents" paid the bills, but they and my oldest sister did not live there. Friends would rotate babysitting so I could attend school during the day and work full-time at night to ensure that I graduated.

2 Timothy 1:8 says, "So do not be ashamed of the testimony about our Lord or of me his prisoner. Rather, join with me in suffering for the gospel, by the power of God." I kept this part of my story to myself. I have loved ones who still do not know some of these details. I was ashamed; God was not. He knew the plans He had for my story. He is the "author and finisher of our faith." **Hebrews 12:2**

Incompetence: And Then I Lost Myself

I gave my life to Christ as a young adult while dating a physically abusive man. By the grace of God and stern instructions from my daddy, I ended that relationship. Quickly! Scars and trauma neatly packed, I went to live with my daddy. Life was good. I could breathe.

I even enrolled in college. The only problem was I did not know how to exist with the ease I yearned for. I was used to dysfunction, and I went back to that which was suffocating me.

Two years after moving back with my mother, I married my now ex-husband. Before marriage, he promised to make me a "good Muslim wife. I did not have enough discernment then to understand how prophetic that statement was to my impending identity loss. I wanted the stability and security he provided. I did whatever he wanted, including converting to Islam. I did not believe in Islam. Hell, I did not believe in me. In hindsight, though, the conversion had nothing to do with him. It concerned my lack of belief in myself and my yearning for stability, security, and love. In our 22-year marriage, we separated for about two years. During that separation, I converted back to Christianity. I hit the ground running, did not look back, and am not tired yet.

Impactful: I Am a Vessel

In April 2007, I moved to Durham, NC. Since I did not know anyone, I spent much of my time alone. Doctors said I could not have children again without medical intervention, yet God gave me sons. I was hired for jobs for which I did not apply or have all the qualifications. God planted people in my life who became my family. Most importantly, God authored my vision. I could see what was happening in my life for the first time. His vision called me to ministry. He called me to marketplace ministry, and my story would be the conduit. **Proverbs 4:7** teaches, "Wisdom is the principal thing: therefore, get wisdom: and in all thy getting get understanding." I knew there was something to my story when a minister critiqued one of my sermonettes by saying, "No one needs to know that you were molested." When I rebutted with **Revelations 12:11,** "And they overcame by the blood of the Lamb and the word of their testimony," the head pastor responded, "You are too young in ministry to know stuff like that.

You still have Similac on your breath." Wisdom taught me their attempt to silence me was an indication of the impact of my story.

I continue to heal each time I share my story. I am not ashamed of my mother's drug addiction. I am not ashamed of being sexually abused. I am not ashamed of being a parentified child. I am not ashamed of being promiscuous. I am not. Hamed of being a teen mom. Each experience allows me to connect with and hold space for others with similar traumas. I undoubtedly know that God also heals whoever hears it.

I am a vessel for God because of my story. God created everything with multiple functionalities; vessels are no different. They can pour out (give) and be poured into (receive). If we quantify ourselves only by what we must provide, we will always miss what we can receive. We will misjudge, misrepresent, and misunderstand who we are, what we are, and why we exist, which is a disservice to everyone, especially God. So…. as you can see, *"I Know Why the Caged Bird Sings."*

For this reason, I AM totally loving my story.

Takia Lovette

"They triumphed over him by the blood of the Lamb and by the word of their testimony; they did not love their lives so much as to shrink from death."
Revelation 12:11 (NIV

Totally Lovin My Story

Write a affirmation for Totally Lovin My Story

_____
_____
_____
_____

What steps will you take to Totally Love Your Story?

_____
_____
_____
_____
_____
_____
_____
_____

What does that look like?

_____
_____
_____
_____

Reflection

Totally Lovin My Story

List 3 take aways from this chapter.

_____
_____
_____
_____
_____
_____
_____

Write a prayer about Totally Lovin My Story

_____
_____
_____
_____
_____
_____
_____
_____

I'M TOTALLY LOVIN MY

Totally Lovin My Differences

Author

Nicole Johnson

ABOUT THE AUTHOR

Nicole Johnson

Coco J (Nicole Johnson) is a dynamic entrepreneur, master stylist, and author dedicated to empowering women in business. With a passion for mentorship, she shares invaluable experiences and insights to help elevate women to new heights. Beyond her professional pursuits, she has a deep love for food, particularly cooking, which allows her to express creativity and joy in the kitchen. Above all, she is guided by a strong faith and a commitment to the Lord, inspiring others to find their own purpose and passion.

www.cocoj.com

TOTALLY LOVIN MY

Differences

By Nicole Johnson

As I sit and reflect on qualities, I have the one that makes me uniquely and WONDERFULLY made. I cannot help but think of a time when my thought process would have allowed me to fully appreciate nor be able to give thanks for the characteristics that make me who I am.

We, especially as women, and even more so as women of color, have inherited certain beliefs and behaviors from the previous generations. We have learned that if we can identify differences between ourselves and others that do not appeal to our personal standard, we can use those differences to criticize, pick a part, or for tearing down. Thinking this will have others appear as weak or less than ourselves. We have chosen to go to WAR with our sisters, wielding our differences like a weapon of mass destruction, leaving behind a trail of emotional damage and unfulfilled potential.

I understand what it means to be both the recipient and the perpetrator of such treatment. I was raised in a household where playing the dozens or joking was used in a veiled attempt to teach you to have tough skin. Hidden behind these jokes and jabs were the distorted views and hidden feelings of someone who was supposed to LOVE ME. I was called everything but a child of God. Things like "High Yellow, Nappy Headed, or Fat." I was always told that I was too much, too loud, too bold, too blunt. While simultaneously being told that I was not enough. I was not smart enough, strong enough, or good enough. I was deemed naive, overly trusting, and too kind. These judgments took on the perception of truth whilst I looked through the lens being placed upon me - the lens of self-hatred and negativity.

There is a saying that what does not kill you makes you stronger, but I do not necessarily agree. Instead, I became hardened, less trusting, and more critical not just of others, but of myself. I became both the criminal and the victim, trapped in the same mindset. I started to see myself through the negative lens which had been spoken to me. This brought about doubting myself and believing the negative words being spoken to me. Thus, slowly killing the potential person I could have been.

The Bible teaches us that as we think, so we become, and that life and death are in the power of the tongue. These two statements are closely intertwined for me.

The lens through which I viewed myself changed everything. I saw the world and myself from a negative and self-doubting perspective.

How many of us are wearing these tainted glasses? How many of us are looking through lenses that have distorted our perception of ourselves and the world around us? Better yet, we are passing these lenses down to our children like some treasured family heirloom. Teaching them to point out what they deem inferior in a way that not only alters their own identity but also damages others in the process. I certainly hope not.

Today, I proudly declare that **I wholeheartedly love my DIFFERENCES!!!**

I have discarded the inherited glasses through which I once saw myself. These glasses were tainted with generational curses and self-doubt. Instead, I have chosen to wear the lens of Christ, and what was once murky and unclear has become clear as crystal.

It is our differences that make us truly unique. I embrace my boldness, my loudness, my honesty, and my capacity to love and forgive. I celebrate the tone of my skin, my raspy voice, and my curly hair. I am confident in my body, my vivaciousness, my quirks, my sense of humor, and my intelligence. I revel in my uniqueness and embrace my identity as a child of The Most High God.

For it is God who has called us into existence, for we are fearfully and wonderfully made! Marvelous are His works, and our worth is far above that of rubies! I now understand that the qualities that set me apart allow me to step into the space that has been uniquely carved out for me with purpose. But it is GOD who makes the greatest DIFFERENCE in our lives.

So, if God made the difference for me and how I viewed myself, I know that he can do the same for you. So, I challenge you, the next time the enemy starts placing in your thoughts to belittle, criticize or judge yourself or someone else, take captive those thoughts, and remind yourself again, and again until it sticks that we are ALL children of the Most High God.

I see your Differences and find them Totally Beautiful!

Nicole Johnson

For you created my inmost being you knit me together in my mother's womb. I praise you because I am fearfully and wonderfully made; your works are wonderful; I know that full well."

Psalm 139:13-14 (NIV)

Totally Lovin My Differences

Write a affirmation for Totally Lovin My Differences

_____

_____

_____

_____

What steps will you take to Totally Love Your Differences ?

_____

_____

_____

_____

_____

_____

_____

What does that look like?

_____

_____

_____

_____

Reflection

Totally Lovin My Differences

List 3 take aways from this chapter.

_____

_____

_____

_____

_____

_____

_____

Write a prayer about Totally Lovin My Differences

_____

_____

_____

_____

_____

_____

_____

_____

I'M TOTALLY LOVIN MY

Totally Lovin
My Servitude

Author

Olivia Turner

ABOUT THE AUTHOR

I'm originally from Huntsville, AL. I obtained my Bachelor's Degree in Music Performance-Piano from Oakwood College in 1988, now Oakwood University in Huntsville, AL. I then received my Master Degree in Speech & Hearing Science from The Ohio State University in Columbus in 1991.

I'm currently practicing as a Speech-Language Pathologist working with elementary and middle school students. I am also a freelance voiceover artist for Mt. Calvary S.D.A Church in the Communications Department, a member of The African American Voice Actors, a freelance playwright, writing plays for Christmas programs and Children's Ministries events.

I am the owner and CEO of OTVOIS LLC, Voice Over International Services

I enjoy playing the piano, singing and praising God on the Mt. Calvary Praise Team. I long to bring people closer to Christ through the talents and gifts He has given me.

TOTALLY LOVIN MY

Servitude

By Olivia Turner

Psalm 100:2-5 King James Version (KJV)

Serve the LORD with gladness: Come before his presence with singing. Know ye that the LORD He is God: It is He that hath made us, and not we ourselves; We are His people, and the sheep of His pasture. Enter His gates with thanksgiving, And into His courts with praise: Be thankful unto Him and bless His name. For the LORD is good; His mercy is everlasting; And His truth endureth to all generations.

When I think of the word servitude, my mind immediately goes to slavery. There was no gladness in slavery. No gladness in being beaten or treated like trash. The slave master was not someone you could confide in or tell your deepest desires. There was no love in being sexually molested or being separated from your family, the ones who loved you the most, most times never seeing them again.

However, when I look at servitude from a biblical standpoint, nothing but love fills my mind. The master we serve is a loving, merciful, gracious Father, who loves me with everlasting love. I can talk to Him about anything. When I mess up, He is there to forgive me and lift me up into His loving arms, telling me that He still loves me.

I grew up in a Christian, God-fearing home. We had family worship, went to church every Saturday, and prayed together about every day. My parents instilled in us the need to have our own relationship with Jesus. They let us kids know that Jesus is always there to help and guide us in the way we should go, even if they as parents were not around. They taught us that Jesus' love never fails. They taught us how to live a life of servitude, serving others, which in turn will bring us all closer to God, hastening His soon coming. However, it was not until I left home to attend grad school that these teachings really came into play.

Growing up, I am one that suffered very badly from low self-esteem. I was always putting myself down, not thinking I was good enough for this or smart enough for that. I was not the smartest person. It took me longer to catch on to various concepts in school than the other students. I had to work harder, study longer, or so it seemed. Growing up and throughout elementary school, and even in high school, I was made fun of over my looks, the shape of my body, my legs, being a late bloomer, my feet, the clothes I wore, etc. It was not until I got to college that I really began liking/loving myself. I did not always share with my parents everything that was happening to me at school.

However, throughout all this low self-esteem it was my family and close friends that kept me going. The love and encouragement shown by my parents, teachers, church, siblings, friends, and extended family sustained me. The early teachings of God's love stuck out. Watching my parents serve the Lord with all their heart, mind, and soul made a permanent imprint on my heart, my whole being. They trusted God with everything, always telling me to pray about everything, no matter the situation.

I find myself now serving God in many capacities. I have held several offices in my local church. But there is so much more to serving God than just holding church offices. I recall the text **1 Cor. 10:31 KJV** which says whether therefore ye eat, or drink, or whatsoever ye do, do all to the glory of God. At first it took me a while to realize this.

In the offices I currently hold, I pray and ask God, "How can I make a difference in leading someone to Christ, by the way I operate in the office(s) I hold?" Serving God not only relates to how I serve my church family, but how I relate to my immediate family as well. Am I being an example of love and kindness? Do they see Jesus in me? What about at my job? Am I making a difference? Do my coworkers see that I operate under a higher power? What kind of servitude legacy am I leaving? Am I one way at church and a different way at home? Do my husband and children see me as a phony? These are the questions that I prayerfully ask myself on a regular basis, which help me stay in check.

Serving the Lord with gladness is not always easy when life's trials are thrown at you left and right. The pressures of life can weigh you down, causing you to lose sight of the ultimate prize that awaits us—Heaven. When we take the focus off ourselves, and focus on serving others, there is a joy that fills our hearts. The other week the children's ministry at my church took on a project of making "Blessing Bags" to be distributed to the homeless.

The joy of making the bags was awesome. Everyone was focused on serving others, those who were less fortunate than we are. There was an even greater joy in passing out the bags. Seeing the joy on the faces of those who received the bags was priceless.

Serving the Lord usually makes me recall a song or songs. Singing brings me joy. I sing on a praise team as well as lead out from time to time. Whenever I lead out, I always pray, asking God, "What songs would You like to hear during this week's praise segment? What songs will touch the hearts of the people the most, turning their hearts toward You? What songs will set the atmosphere of true worship? What songs will make You smile?"

Every time I ask these questions and earnestly seek to find songs to answer these questions, our praise and worship segment lifts the hearts of the congregation, setting us up to receive the blessing from the spoken word of God.

Serving God through music that has been dedicated to Him can be the best remedy to heal a broken heart, bring that peace that surpasses all understanding, mend that broken relationship, and cause someone to give their life to Jesus.

I'd like to end by calling our attention to what God requires of us in **Deuteronomy 10:12** which says, "And now, Israel, what does the LORD your God require of you, but to fear the LORD your God, to walk in all His ways, to love Him, to serve the **LORD your God** with all your heart and with all your soul, **(ESV)**

So yes, I love my servitude to God!

Olivia Turner

"God is not unjust; he will not forget your work and the love you have shown him as you have helped his people and continue to help them."

Hebrews 6:10 (NIV):

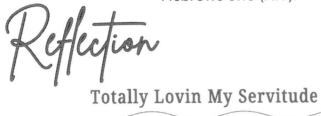 

Totally Lovin My Servitude

Write a affirmation for Totally Lovin My Servitude

_____
_____
_____
_____

What steps will you take to Totally Love Your Servitude?

_____
_____
_____
_____
_____
_____
_____
_____
_____
_____

What does that look like?

_____
_____
_____
_____
_____

Reflection

Totally Lovin My Differences

List 3 take aways from this chapter.

_____

_____

_____

_____

_____

_____

_____

Write a prayer about Totally Lovin My Servitude

_____

_____

_____

_____

_____

_____

_____

_____

I'M TOTALLY LOVIN MY

Totally Lovin My Wins

Author

Apostle Freida Henderson

ABOUT THE AUTHOR

Apostle Freida Henderson

Dr. Freida Henderson Is the mother of three amazing children and a grandmother of five beautiful granddaughters and one handsome grandson.

She is the founder of the Greater Word of Truth Ministry in Garner, North Carolina over 21 years. Dr. Freida's mission is not limited to using her voice and talents to win souls in the body of christ. She also helps people "win" in life. She is a highly sought-after Speaker, Certified Christian Life Coach, and multi-business owner.

The Winning Approach LLC. Where women build their confidence, conquer fears and Discover their passion and dive into their purpose.

Dr Freida is a Best Selling Author that has authored and published several books, as well as helped others become first time authors.

www.thewinningapproach.com

TOTALLY LOVIN MY

Wins

By Dr. Freida Henderson

Victory amid my trials…

"For the Lord, your God is the one who goes with you to fight for you against your enemies to give you victory." **(Deuteronomy 20:4)**

From the very beginning of my life, I had health issues. I was born with a heart defect. I had a hole in my heart, and the doctors said if I did not have open heart surgery, I could die. While on the operating table, I woke up as they were cutting me. That is a pain I will never forget, excruciating pain. During the surgery, I was told my heart stopped beating, and they could not get it started again. It stopped for so long that the doctors said it was possible that I would be a vegetable if I survived.

Thank you, Jesus, I survived the surgery. After the surgery, I had to learn how to walk all over again because the scar was straight down the middle of my chest. I walked hunched over. They told my parents that I would walk hunched over like that for the rest of my life.

My parents were told of all these things that I would not be able to do because of the type of surgery I had. Well, I want you to know I beat all those odds. I was not a vegetable. I began to walk straight, and I was able to run track in school. God had a plan for my life. Man saw it one way, but God planned it another way.

Even though I survived the surgery and beat the odds I still had to go back home to an abusive environment. I was in a home that was financially stable, but the love was not there. But even in that, between the physical and mental abuse I found peace at church even at an early age. I loved going to church. I went to church every Sunday, sang in the choir, and participated in all the youth activities. The reason I mentioned this was because the seeds were planted. I received Jesus Christ as my Lord and Savior at an exceedingly early age. What I did not know then but know now is that "it all" set me up to become who I am today in Christ.

At an early age I knew there was something different about me. I did not know it then but later learned that God had called me to a higher purpose. This would explain the dreams.

I was having of leaving Detroit. It was not just a mere Fantasy but Prophecies of a future Unbound by geographical chains. A true testament to the plans God had laid out for my life.

The true measure of winning "Victory" is often misconstrued as an absence of adversity, but true Victory is finding God's purpose and strength Within those adversities. Winning is not about avoiding the storms, but it is about finding peace amidst the storms. It is about recognizing that help and Hope comes from our unshakable faith in Jesus Christ.

I found my victory in Scripture, and I began to Totally Love My Wins. The scriptures guided me and helped me to see I was not in this alone. These two scriptures quickly became my favorites.

Proverbs 3:5-6 says, "Trust in the Lord with all thine heart and lean not unto thine own understanding. In all thy ways acknowledge Him and He Shall direct thy paths."

Even when I was a young girl and did not really understand the fullness of the Word of God, this scripture spoke to me.

The other scripture that captured me was Romans 8:28 that says, "And we know that all things work together for good to them that love God to them who are called according to his purpose."

It was these two scriptures that helped me to realize that I was a winner and that I was going to win in life. I went through many traumatic situations divorce, loss of jobs and homelessness over the years but I come to tell you that my God saw me through them all. The trajectory of my life shifted aligning more closely with God's purpose revealing victories in places I once marked as defeat.

Totally Loving My Wins. The small and mighty wins. These are times when the small wins far outweighed the Larger than Life wins because they are often the hardest ones to come by but learn how to celebrate the small wins. The days when you handle a difficult conversation with Grace and love. The days when you take time out for yourself and do a little self-care is a win for us women of God because we are always taking care of others. These might not result in immediate recognition or financial gain but trust me they are Wins.

I want to encourage you all that no matter what we go through God has a plan for our lives. He knew us before we were formed in our mother's womb. He had a plan for our life just like Jeremiah 29:11 says, "For I know the plans I have for you declares the Lord plans to prosper you and to not harm you, plans to give you hope and a future."

So, no matter what you face in life, always remember if we are in Jesus Christ we are never alone though the battles and the trials can seem many at times, just remember He promised He would never leave us nor forsake us. We must remember to stand strong and firm in our faith.

1 Corinthians 15:57 says, "But thanks be to God who gives us Victory through our Lord Jesus Christ." Through him, we are more than conquerors and able to overcome the trials and tribulations of this world.

Acknowledging Him deepens our dependency on His divine strength, not just to win battles but to conquer in a manner that glorifies him. **Winning is" Transforming Our victories" into testimonies of His faithfulness and power.**

Apostle Freida Henderson

Devotional

TOTALLY LOVIN MY

WINS

"Fear not, for I am with you; be not dismayed, for I am your God. I will strengthen you; I will help you; I will uphold you with my righteous right hand."

Isaiah 41:10

Devotional

Totally Lovin My Wins

Turning our fear into faith can unlock the strength we need to overcome challenges. Though you may not always see His hand, take comfort in knowing He is always there, guiding you towards victory.

PRAYER

Heavenly Father, thank You for the victories, big and small, that fill my life with purpose and joy. Help me to celebrate each win as a reminder of Your faithfulness and the gifts You've placed within me. May I stay humble in success, giving You the glory, and may each win inspire me to keep striving and growing in Your love. In Jesus' name, Amen

Reflection

Totally Lovin My Wins

Write a affirmation for Totally Lovin My Wins

_____
_____
_____
_____

What steps will you take to Totally Lovin My Wins

_____
_____
_____
_____
_____
_____
_____
_____

What does that look like?

_____
_____
_____
_____
_____

Reflection
Totally Lovin My Differences

List 3 take aways from this chapter.

_____

_____

_____

_____

_____

_____

_____

Write a prayer about Totally Lovin My Wins

_____

_____

_____

_____

_____

_____

_____

_____

I'M TOTALLY LOVIN MY

Totally Lovin My Journey

Author
Apostle Totlisa Vereen

ABOUT THE AUTHOR

Apostle Totlisa Vereen

I am a wife, a mother of three, and a YaYa. Above all, I am a child of God. My journey has been amazing, and there is nothing that I would change. Every experience is a learning experience, and this journey has taught and shown me so much. I live on purpose for a purpose.

TOTALLY LOVIN MY

Journey

By Totlisa Vereen

I have not always loved this journey. I came from a one-parent home and did not know where my father was or even if he was alive. Molested by different men and told to stay quiet so it does not hurt anyone else. I did not particularly like my appearance, so I always covered myself, thinking that if I were not noticeable, I could escape the eyes of others. Having no father and being molested by men gave me low self-esteem. I felt unworthy, lost, ashamed, stolen, taken advantage of, unloved, bound, confused, and always questioned why.

I got pregnant and had a daughter in my junior year of high school. I had a teacher who encouraged me to quit because she said it was shameful to be pregnant in school. But I just could not quit. I had so much to prove to her and others. By my senior year, I was so scared and worried about others' opinions of me that I hid my second pregnancy and gave birth five months after graduating.

Carrying the weight of being a young, single mother of two and facing life challenges itself applied more pressure on top of issues, trials, and tribulations. I chose not to abort my second child. I was told that neither his father nor his grandparents would ever accept him. It was hard to grasp because they accepted my first child. My son went without his biological father until the age of twenty-one. My life began to change when I felt God had sent me a man who would accept me and my children as his own. The thing I longed for was the love, peace, and commitment he fulfilled. This he taught and showed me love unconditionally and how a woman should be cared for by a man.

Looking back, I remember losing my mother at the age of twenty-one and instantly having to raise my two children along with the responsibility of taking care of my three siblings. This was not easy. And the question of why arose again.

After one year of dating, I married my current husband. I was only twenty-two, still a baby with babies, and now a wife. Two years later, away from home, I still felt lost, fearful, doubtful, and ashamed. Trying to make the best of it, building memories good and some not so good. Yet they are the memories that I was trying to use to block out my childhood trauma and drama. The old was never dealt with or allowed to be buried so that new life could begin. There were traumas that were covered and suppressed. The scarring of the old memories and trying to manage the new brought depression, insecurities, shame, loneliness, rejection, bondage, and questions with no answers. I could never see the fullness of myself and what I was created to be.

Time passed, days went by, months, years, and seasons changed, but my journey was still mine. I could not understand what was coming, what to look for, or how it would end. I thank GOD for being a FATHER of second and even third chances as I gave my life to him multiple times and still came up short. In my shortcomings, he never took his hands off me and the purpose he has for my life. I did not understand then, but I know I was created with a purpose to do his will and carry out his plan. I came into a place of truly seeking a man who would change my life forever.

I was no longer held in a place of unforgiveness against myself and others. I was free from any bondage, chains, and shackles of my past, hurts, traumas, drama, trials, or tribulations. No longer was I in that place of rejection from man but in a place of being loved with unfailing love from GOD. I was snatched by the hands of my creator to know that I was perfectly made in his image. I did not have to look like others, nor did I any longer hate how I looked. I was becoming and embracing my inward beauty.

I had to get to Totally Lovin' Me to get Totally Lovin' My Journey. I would not change the beginning of my walk, my endurance, my lack, my rejection, nor my misunderstandings. What I thought was sent to hurt me, GOD turned it around for my good and his glory.

Jeremiah 29:11(KJV) says, "For I know the thoughts that I think toward you, saith the Lord, thoughts of peace, and not of evil, to give you an expected end."

I know how to love the unlovable and forgive even when no apologies exist. I learned how not to walk in unforgiveness. After forty-five years, I was able to be in a relationship with my biological father, his family, and my three siblings. I have three healthy children and six grandchildren who call me Yaya. I have a wonderful husband with whom I do ministry. He walks with me and encourages me to continue moving forward. He is my biggest cheerleader. GOD has been showing himself to be mighty in the things concerning my family and me. My breakdowns were preparing me for my breakthrough and coming forth.

My journey will never compare to the journey that **JESUS** took so that I will have eternal life.

My journey was never over; it was just getting started. I love this amazing journey. I came into Totally Lovin' My Journey. I had to start somewhere. I did not know or understand the middle, but I now know there is greater at the end. I am ready and expecting to see it all.

Remember that your latter days shall be greater. As you are on your journey, no matter what point you are at, always know that it is not how you start but how you finish. Chin Up, Crown Fixed, Warrior Ready, and Stance Undefeated. As GOD has done it for me, HE will do it for You. Finish strong, at the end... Love Your Journey.

Totally Lovin MY JOURNEY

Apostle Totlisa Vereen

"For whatever was written in former days was written for our instruction, that through endurance and the encouragement of the Scriptures we might have hope."

Romans 15:4

Reflection
Totally Lovin My Journey

Write a affirmation for Totally Lovin My Journey

_____

_____

_____

What steps will you take to Totally Love Your Journey?

_____

_____

_____

_____

_____

_____

_____

What does that look like?

_____

_____

_____

_____

Reflection

Totally Lovin My Journey

List 3 take aways from this chapter.

_____

_____

_____

_____

_____

_____

_____

_____

Write a prayer about Totally Lovin My Journey

_____

_____

_____

_____

_____

_____

_____

_____

I'M TOTALLY LOVIN MY

Totally Lovin My Uniqueness

Author

Dr. Cathy Jennings

ABOUT THE AUTHOR
Dr. Cathy Jennings

I am Dr. Cathy Jennings, often referred to as Dr. J. Originally from Greenwood, South Carolina, I hold a PhD in Theology with a focus on Christian Counseling, and I am a professional Life Coach. Currently, I teach at the ROLTC School of Revelation, founded by Apostle Donna Pierce. I developed the "Healthy Mind: Developing and Equipping a Sober Mind" series as well as the "Not All Wounds are Visible" curriculum. With twenty-three years of experience in Public and Behavioral Education, I also possess a Master of Arts in Management and Leadership and Human Resources Management from Webster University. As a certified Career and Educational Life Coach, I am passionate about inspiring and empowering others to become the best versions of themselves. My diverse background includes supervisory roles, public speaking, mentorship, and the implementation of policies, practices, and recruitment strategies within a business context.

Above all, my love for Jesus is paramount. My greatest passion lies in praising and worshiping God. I have been involved in singing in various forms since I was fourteen, beginning my journey at True Vine Progressive Church of Jesus under the leadership of Pastor Paul Jennings Sr. Currently, I serve as the Praise and Worship Leader at New Day Community Church, where Pastor Richard D. Hayes guides us. My philosophy is simple: I don't want to just exist; I strive to be a blessing wherever I go.

TOTALLY LOVIN MY

Uniqueness

By Dr. Cathy Jennings

The **UNIQUENESS OF ME**...I am reminded of the scripture where it says in Psalms 139:14 which says " I am fearfully and wonderfully made. For years, I neglected to see being wonderfully made" because I was the "Black Sheep '. The uniqueness was merely in the black sheep.

I can remember it being said "You think you are better than someone else" I was considered a bookworm because I applied statistics, terminology, data, rhetoric, and principles in most I do. A common question I am asked is "Why are you in school now" and" What degree are you working on now." The number of degrees I have has been thrown in my face in numerous conversations. Even Paul in the Bible knew how to operate in his many citizenships. I have been chosen as a **"BLACK SHEEP,"** yet **TOTALLY LOVIN, the UNIQUENESS of ME!!!!**

What are "black sheep"?

The term black sheep is sometimes connected with negative connotations. A black sheep is considered a scapegoat for others' mischief, strange, weird, peculiar, unconventional, worthless, they are always up to some type of foolishness, a troublemaker and misunderstood. They are made to feel as though they will never line up with the values, beliefs, and norms of others such as family, group, church family associates, and colleagues. Even black sheep were mentioned in the Bible.

Genesis 38:1-30.

If you have ever taken an interest in genealogy and family history, chances are you have run into some "black sheep." They are the sort of people that your relatives are either eager to gossip about or whose mention causes them to fall into silence. Many uses black sheep to distract their subconscious mind from their own trauma, mindsets, behaviors, generational **curses, and biases.**

Signs that you have been chosen to be black sheep or ostracized:

- Do you find yourself on the outside looking in?
- Are constantly being criticized or judged for your natural attributes; such as your educational level, ideas, opinions, ideas, and beliefs?
- Are you bullied by those in cliches?
- Have you heard it said, "Don't act like them or we don't want you to end up or act like ____(insert your name)."
- Do you find yourself seeking support from others outside the people you are around and interact with?
- When you strive to achieve a goal, get stronger and more independent breaking generational curses, you sense others intent on bringing you down or dismissing any or all your achievements.

Black Sheep!!! Survive!!! Black Sheep!!!Thrive!!!

If you were the black sheep of the family, you might have gone through a lot of personal reflection, therapy, and healing to get to where you are, despite the shame, guilt, and trauma you were made to carry. Jesus said, b**y "HIS STRIPES YOU ARE HEALED."**

You must embrace your unique you! In **Jeremiah 1:5**" Before I made you in your mother's womb, I chose you." God chose you to be distinctive. Unique means being the only one of its kind; unlike anything else. Can you imagine opening a box of twenty-four crayons and all the crayons are purple? A box of purple crayons is useful, but a box with assorted colors provides diversity. Each color whether red, yellow, blue, black, or white has a purpose. Each color brings a distinct view to a picture or display.

I can remember the time when people told me my voice was loud when I sang. The microphone has been privately turned down on me as if I did not know. I believe in following peace with all men so I would let the tears run down my face and not say a word. My goal was not to intentionally have a loud voice or to annoy anyone. I wanted to sing to bring God, and glory, honor. I give him thanks for all my gifts.

I cannot count the number of times " I love to hear someone say" ____ (insert someone else name) sing. I thought the fix to the matter was to pray and ask God to lower my voice. Singing became a burden and not a gift.

I had surgery on my tonsils, adenoids, and nostrils a few weeks after that prayer. Let me tell you, I got the answer to my prayer, and I did not like it. For over six months I could not speak clearly, let alone sing for people to understand me. Jesus gave me just what I asked for. I learned two valuable lessons. First, be careful that for which you pray. Second, be careful how you pray. After my throat and nose had healed, I never complained to Jesus or worried about what others had to say. I knew my voice was a part of my **Unique ME Jeremiah 29:11 "** For I know the plans I have for you."

Spiritual Nuggets and Lessons of Being the Black Sheep

Finally, there are seven spiritual nuggets of being the black sheep. First, you can cultivate your inner circle. As the black sheep, you will disconnect, self-isolate, and become a loner. This allows you to cultivate your circle. Being alone gives the opportunity for self-reflection and helps you access the deep crevices of your soul that will hibernate in the distraction of social interactions in this world.

Secondly, black sheep are usually timid, shy, pushovers, and can easily be made to doubt their point of view. It is time to recognize your unique point of view. Since it is not the common way of perceiving the world, we live in.

When you recognize your uniqueness, YOU are a gift versus a source of pain. It is the beginning of healing the hurt. We must practice listening to ourselves, our voices, our dreams, and our perspectives.

Thirdly, we must learn to use our voice. In Ecclesiastes 3: 7-8 it says "a time to rend, and a time to sew; a time to keep silence, and a time to speak; a time to love, and a time to hate; a time of war, and a time of peace. Being unique comes with the profound responsibility to share it with others.

Challenge yourself to be understood. "We cannot hide behind, "People just do not' get me" anymore. We develop our spiritual opportunities only by practicing using a voice that challenges us to be understood by those who "used to" intimidate us. Being understood requires us to master our skills. It requires us to understand and highlight our unique point of view to such a high degree that when you speak, you will be surprised who will start to listen.

Next, we must heal the wounds that make us fearful to connect with others. When we live in a trap that prevents us from connecting with others because we perceive they will not understand. We hurt ourselves and withhold what's precious that Jesus Christ has given us. To shift this, there needs to be a conscious decision to heal these beliefs. Ponder on Philippians 4:13, "I CAN DO ALL THIS THROUGH CHRIST WHO STRENGTHENS.

CONCLUSION OF THE MATTER: SPEAK LIFE!!

1. I am DIFFERENT and that is OK.
2. I MATTER to the KINGDOM.
3. I have a VOICE!
5. I am WONDERFULLY MADE.
6. I will be kind and LOVE on MYSELF today.
7. I will TAKE ACTIONS.

Dr. Cathy Jennings

"The stone the builders rejected has become the cornerstone."
Psalm 118:22 (NIV)

Totally Lovin My Uniqueness

Write a affirmation for Totally Lovin My Uniqueness

_____

_____

_____

What steps will you take to Totally Love Your Uniqueness?

_____

_____

_____

_____

_____

_____

_____

What does that look like?

_____

_____

_____

_____

_____

Reflection

Totally Lovin My Uniqueness

List 3 take aways from this chapter.

_____

_____

_____

_____

_____

_____

_____

_____

_____

Write a prayer about Totally Lovin My Uniqueness

_____

_____

_____

_____

_____

_____

_____

_____

I'M TOTALLY LOVIN MY

Totally Lovin My
Step By Step Walk

Author

Dr. Patricia Coleman

ABOUT THE AUTHOR

Dr. Patricia Coleman

Apostle, Dr. Patricia Coleman is the pastor of Perfect Love Ministries in MABANK Texas. She is the author of a book called "Broken Pieces" She is the wife of Bishop Reginald Coleman of 38 years.

Dr. Patricia is the mother of two biological children. They have been blessed to raise three children of their own, and enjoy the life of a blended family. Dr. Patricia Coleman is passionate about serving God and his people.

TOTALLY LOVIN MY

Step By Step Walk

By Dr. Patricia Coleman

This is what gives me the courage to walk out the path that God has set before me. It is the mere fact that God has a glorious destination awaiting me. He continues to show me that as I walk out this natural life, in the life of the spirit, things will begin to evolve and come to life. I do not believe we are meant to stumble and fumble our way through life, it is God 's will that we walk purposefully, consistently in the direction of God 's best for us. **Eph 5:15** says "Be careful then, how you walk, not as unwise but as wise.

Eph. 2:2 says we are not to walk according to the World.
Your step-by-step walk is your manner of life. Your character following Jesus is a daily walk I often say that the world is watching not our Words but our walk. The power of your faith is really in your daily steps. Your actions are where the rubber meets the road. Your faith is not in how loud you shout on Sunday but in how you walk throughout the week.

I often find myself looking and asking God about my step-by-step walk. I long to understand God's grand vision for my life. I desire to see clearly, walk out the path to get to where you desire me to be.

Step-by-step walk with God is when I realize his ultimate love and acceptance for me. I recognize my "true identity" in him as I discovered I was built and designed for this. I had no idea what it meant to really walk with God. The concept was foreign, distant like a Misty haze of fog along the horizon.

ABBA, you are not a man that you should lie, I want to know you more. I want to see your promises to me come to pass. (Such a simple prayer of heartfelt and openness.)

The invitation of the unknown God before me Catapulted my entire existence in a way I can hardly even begin to describe, and it still feels like we have not landed.

We can confidently walk with God through the trials of life step-by-step one day at a time we will make this journey.

The Lord has brought me through the treacherous terrain of fears realized and shown me that I can walk through fire when I walk with him. I still fear the burns from time to time but the more we go through this life together step-by-step he reveals that I do not have to be afraid because he is with me.

He is with me. Words, they carry so much more weight after walking together through a few storms. Had I understood in the beginning that the Christian Walk is a process of unfolding, I think I would have been able to offer myself quite a bit more grace and compassion in the earlier years.

You see faith is not unlike any relationship, it starts with two people getting to know each other and that process unfolds step-by-step over the course of time. A walk with God is not for the faint of heart. There is no way to simplify the faith walk, you must take the steps to truly appreciate the grandeur of it all.

Step-by-step we will make this journey. The enemy's agenda is to make you feel afraid, isolated, and fearful of beginning your journey with Christ, but he is a liar. There are benefits with the journey of knowing Christ.

So, let me ask you how are you walking in your walk with Christ? Are you consistent are inconsistent? Does your walk reveal a daily trust in God, or do you follow your own way? Are you prayerful? Are you faithful? Are you humbled? Are you loving? Your opinions do not matter as much as your life example.

Improve your life one step at a time, nobody has the perfect life. I am sure everyone wants to change their mindset and lifestyle, so we must work on ourselves daily. It is easy to change your life just take it step-by-step. Each week try a new step, take it slow, because it does not all need to be done in a day and Live your Best Life!

Dr. Patricia Coleman

Devotional

TOTALLY LOVIN MY

STEP BY STEP WALK

I have discovered through the year that God leads us one step at a time. His promises are: "As you go step-by-step, I will open up the way before you."

Proverbs 4:12 (Literal Translation)

Devotional

Totally Lovin My
Step By Step Walk

Observation:

Improve your life one step at a time. No one has the perfect life. Your step-by-step walk with God is when you realize his ultimate love and acceptance for you.

PRAYER

Heavenly Father,

I thank You for walking with me through every step of life's journey. Help me to trust Your plan, even when the path seems unclear. Teach me to embrace the process, knowing that each step brings me closer to Your perfect will. May I find peace in Your love and acceptance, growing stronger with every move forward. In Jesus' name, Amen.

Dr. Patricia Coleman

Reflection

Totally Lovin My Step By Step Walk

Write a affirmation for Totally Lovin Your Step By Step Walk

_____

_____

_____

_____

What steps will you take for your Step By Step Walk?

_____

_____

_____

_____

_____

_____

What does that look like?

_____

_____

_____

_____

Reflection

Totally Lovin My Step By Step Walk

List 3 take aways from this chapter.

_____

_____

_____

_____

_____

_____

_____

_____

Write a prayer that will help you Totally Lovin My Step By Step Walk

_____

_____

_____

_____

_____

_____

_____

_____

_____

I'M TOTALLY LOVIN MY

Totally Lovin My Identity

Author

Dora Rice

ABOUT THE AUTHOR

Minister Dora Rice is a native of West Virginia and serves under the leadership of Apostle Sterling V. Porter III at Kingdom Life Cathedral Ministries located in Charles Town, WV. She has recorded music projects such as "All My Worship" and "You Fight For Me". Minister Dora has traveled the world ministering the gospel of Jesus Christ and has served in missions in the country of Uganda.

She is the author of "Mirror Mirror, A Case of Identity Thief". She has also co-authored books such as" She Held Me Up" and "No Longer Broken". Minister Dora has been featured in Totally Lovin' Me Magazine, interviewed for Quotidien Television in France, Dominion TV, and has been named one of the Top 23 Women to Watch in 2023 Edition in Totally Lovin' Me Magazine.

Dora Rice's prophetic gifting has led to overcome obstacles the enemy has placed in her path to derail her purpose and destiny. She is able to withstand his temptation with power and authority because of her close proximity to God and His anointing on her life. She shares her testimony all over the world,because she is free, and loves to witness others experience the same. The freedom only God can produce."

www.doraministries.com

FB Personal: Dora Rice
FB Ministry: Dora Ministries
IG: doraministries

TOTALLY LOVIN MY

Identity

By Dora Rice

When I, you, we were born into this world we were born innocent... full of life... imagination... full of dreams... and the possibilities seem endless...

Then as we begin this journey called life, we may have had dreams of becoming a doctor, lawyer, international superstar, actor, writer, wife, husband, mother, father... The list could go on and on. We had no limits, no boundaries. Anything seemed possible and attainable. Then the reality of life sets in... with all its difficulties... pains and triumphs... achievements and disappointments, something in us begins to change...

Perhaps, it was the moment of abuse or misuse that made our world seem smaller than it once was. Or could it be the generational curses of financial hardship and instability that made our once possible dreams become impossible to attain? Maybe it was the choices we made in our lives that caused us to feel unworthy or less than. Always comparing ourselves, instead of believing that we were and are worth believing again... starting again... living again?

As life happens and our environment and people (yes, I said people) begin to shape us, we start to take on the identity that someone else thinks we should have... we begin to view ourselves through the distorted lenses of having to live up to our parents' expectations... society's expectations... what Hollywood says we should be... what "religion" says we can or cannot be comparing ourselves to others and others successes... and it begins to change us...

We eventually stepped away from that child that dreamed big and thought the world had no limit. We stop believing we could be anything we wanted, go anywhere, and do everything of which we could dream. As we walk further and further away from our childhood and walk into adulthood, we allow our surroundings and the voices of influence in our lives to change us.

We no longer live the life we dreamed of so long ago, but we live the life that someone else shapes us to believe we want, which most of the time is the life those people around us wish they would have lived but since they didn't fulfill their dreams are now trying to accomplish it through us.

We begin to take on a false identity and be shaped into someone other than who God created us to be because of who we have surrounded ourselves with and who we have allowed to speak into our lives. We follow their leadership because we feel they know what is best for us; however, only to have forgotten that we were and always will be created and shaped in His likeness.

The Bible says in **Colossians 1:16-20 (NKJV)**
16 For by Him all things were created that are in heaven and that are on earth, visible and invisible, whether thrones or dominions or [a]principalities or [b]powers. All things were created through Him and for Him.

And in Genesis 1:26a (NKJV)
26 Then God said, "Let Us make man in Our image, according to Our likeness.

God is calling us to come back to the original identity and design of who He created us to be. He is calling us to walk in the authority given to us as His sons and daughters. No longer do we need to struggle with our identity because that identity is found in Christ. The road may seem long, but it is worth it. God has freed us to rule and reign with Him. We have that kind of power because of who He is and who we are in relationship with Him.

The enemy is good at distorting our view of how we look at ourselves. He causes us to take on the identity of what we have done or who others have labeled us as being instead of what the Word of God says we are. He has a way of twisting and turning the view of ourselves until we do not even know who we "thought" we were.

No matter where you are reading this book, I want you to look through the lenses of God's eyes and see yourself the way He sees you... Beautiful, Wonderfully Made, The Apple of His Eye, His Daughter, His Son. He loves you more than you could ever imagine.

So, if we were created in the image of God and are the apple of His eye, we should combat the enemy with the Word of God that would dispel every lie that tells us that we are struggling with our identity. We are free to go back and reclaim our father's original blueprint for our lives.

Here are some scriptures to remind you of who God says you are:

2 Corinthians 5:17 calls you a new creation

John 5:16 declares you are chosen.

Ephesians 2:19 calls you a citizen of the Kingdom

Psalm 45:11 declares you are beautiful.

Ephesians 2:10 calls you special

Jeremiah 29:11 declares you were created for a purpose.

Psalm 18:35 declares you are strong.

Psalm 13:12 declares you are forgiven.

Galatians 4:7 declares you are free.

Discovering Who I am!

The scripture is specific about who God created us to be and proposed us for. The following list of scriptures shares many of those thoughts our Daddy God has about us. They show how He identifies us. I encourage you to post them around your home and read them as declarations daily.

I have eternal life because I believe in the son **(John 3:36)**

I have peace **(John 14:27)**

I am loved by Jesus **(John 15:9)**

I am loved by the father **(John 16:27) (Ephesians 2:4)**

I belong to God **(John 17:9)**

Jesus is in me **(John 17:23**

I have forgiveness of sins **(Acts 13:38**

I have been freed from all things **(ACTS 13:39)**

I have peace with God through Jesus Christ **(Romans 5:1)**

I have been justified by His blood **(Romans 5:9)**

I reign in life through Jesus **(Romans 5:17)**

I walk in newness of life **(Romans 6:4)**

I am led by the Spirit of God, I'm a child of God.

(Romans 8:14)

I am called of God. I am justified in Him **(Romans 8:30)**

I am never to be separated from the love of God **(Romans 8:38-**

39)

I have been given grace and favor by God.

(I Corinthians 1:4)

I am not lacking any gift **(I Corinthians 1:5)**

I have the mind of Christ **(I Corinthians:16)**

I am the temple of God **(I Corinthians 3:16)**

I belong to Christ **(I Corinthians 3:23)**

I have been bought with a price **(I Corinthians 6:20)**

In short, you are God's image walking the earth. You have all power and authority given to you because you are children of the one true and living King. So, grab ahold of that.
identity and watch the miraculous happen!

You are free to love your identity!

Dora Rice

"Therefore, if anyone is in Christ, the new creation has come: The old has gone, the new is here!

2 Corinthians 5:17 (NIV)

Reflection

Totally Lovin My Identity

Write a affirmation for Totally Lovin My Identity

_____

_____

_____

What steps will you take for your Identitiy?

_____

_____

_____

_____

_____

_____

_____

What does that look like?

_____

_____

_____

_____

Reflection

Totally Lovin My Identity

List 3 take aways from this chapter.

_____

_____

_____

_____

_____

_____

_____

_____

Write a prayer that will help you Totally Lovin Your Identity

_____

_____

_____

_____

_____

_____

_____

_____

I'M TOTALLY LOVIN MY

Totally Lovin My Eyes

Author
Angela Agurs

ABOUT THE AUTHOR

Angela Agurs

Born and raised in Hinesville, Georgia, I'm the second oldest of six siblings. After working as a certified nursing assistant, I pursued a passion for education, earning an Associate Degree in Public Services and Early Childhood Education, followed by a Bachelor's of Science in Early Education Leadership. Now a mother of four and a case manager for the state of South Carolina, my life took another turn in 2014 when I became an ordained minister, embracing the wisdom of the quote, "We cannot conquer today's giants with yesterday's strategies."

TOTALLY LOVIN MY

Eyes

By Angela Agurs

S ome say that eyes are the window to a person's soul, and they tell you everything you need to know. If that statement held any truth, then my eyes told me everything I did not want to know, and the mirror was confirmation of my most negative thoughts. As a teen, I remembered looking at a reflection of someone that I didn't view as pretty, from small eyes, that afforded others to tease me and call me Chinese as some kind of insult, to a big nose which was the biggest feature on my round pie face as my mother would often say. Unfortunately, mirrors come in all sizes, so not only my upper body but also my lower body was subject to self-criticism. However, my perception of my body reflected on glass surfaces was the least of my worries compared to the body shaming of the neighborhood boys who verbalized all my insecurities.

The event that impacted me the most and when the seed of low self-esteem was sown was my experience being molested by individuals on both my mother and father's side of the family. Little did I know that very seed would grow, flourish, and shape areas of my life including my marriage.

October 9, 1998, was the day I married what I wanted to be the love of life. As we prepared our wedding vows to be said in front of a judge, I heard a voice say, "Don't marry him" three times and at that time I did not know it was the Holy Spirit speaking to me. Initially, I began to shake, and my sister jokingly said that I had gotten scared, but against the chilling warning of the soft-spoken voice, which I ignored, I became a married woman. From the marriage, I bore three beautiful children and accepted and embraced a bonus daughter as though she were my own.

Even though my husband was at home, I still felt like a single parent, and to make matters worse, I endured multiple affairs and verbal and mental abuse. I was often belittled for not working and heard things like he should have known he could not turn a whore into a housewife. He would threaten to send me back to where he had found me. The words he uttered clung to me and reminded me that he had saved me from the generational bondage and curse that was spoken over the women of the family that we would bear children but never marry.

The reality of my situation hit me all too fast and hard. I did not have a job, no further education beyond high school, and a nursing assistant certificate that I had let go. How would I be able to support my children? I dreaded the thought of moving back home because what would everyone have to say?

Despite all the odds stacked against me, I made the decision to leave my husband after finding a hotel receipt in the back seat of the car as we were heading to a football game to watch our daughter cheer. I went to Texas with my cousin, but my stay only lasted eight months after my husband convinced me that he realized his mistakes, wanted his family, and was willing to walk into what the Lord had called him to do on the premise that several people had prophesied to him that he had a calling on his life to be a preacher.

The sunshine would be clouded over when the affairs continued a year after I had returned to South Carolina. Coming home late at night or early in the morning began again with the only justification of "I don't have to explain anything to you" or "I don't want to be married to you." As it became darker and darker around me, I began hearing the words, "Just end it; you're not smart enough nor pretty enough; there's nothing you can do here." Those words became my truth, and I took several pills as it was what I thought was my only way to stop the pain of my marriage, of the experiences of my childhood being molested, and of everything I thought made me not worthy or enough to be loved.

I remembered my sister banging on the bathroom door; my husband had called her because I would not let him in. When she came into the bathroom, she began to pray and pour into my spirit, and on that day, I gave my heart to Jesus. I remember praying to God not to let me die and being afraid to fall asleep because I did not know what the result would be from taking the pills. Although I was not able to see myself as God saw me, I began my healing process, allowing myself to heal from childhood trauma and hurt not only as an adult but also as the little girl who lived subconsciously in my mind and heart.

As I transitioned into a single woman and a single parent, I began to see the image in the mirror completely differently. Now I was totally loving what I saw through my eyes and loving the person as God sees. I could see the beauty of my small eyes, round face, and big nose and embrace my body shape. I walked boldly across the stage to receive my associate's degree and eventually found my own foundation and became a homeowner.

For the individual who reads this book and can relate, I pray that God covers you with his unconditional love, his unfailing hands, and his perfect peace. The inspiration and the healing of my life story comes from the following scriptures:

Psalm 139:14 (KJV)-I will praise thee; for I am fearfully and wonderfully made. Wonderful are your works; my soul knows it very well.

Isaiah 41:10 (NLT)- Do not be afraid, for I am with you. Do not be discouraged, for I am your God. I will strengthen you and help you. I will hold you up with my victorious right hand.

Romans 8:28 (NLT)- And we know that God causes everything to work together for the good of those who love God and are called according to his purpose for them.

I am totally loving my eyes!

Angela Agurs

"Therefore, if anyone is in Christ, the new creation has come: The old has gone, the new is here!

2 Corinthians 5:17 (NIV)

Reflection
Totally Lovin My Eyes

Write a affirmation for Totally Lovin My Eyes

_____

_____

_____

_____

What steps will you take to Totally Love Your Eyes?

_____

_____

_____

_____

_____

_____

_____

_____

What does that look like?

_____

_____

_____

_____

_____

Reflection

Totally Lovin My Eyes

List 3 take aways from this chapter.

_____

_____

_____

_____

_____

_____

_____

Write a prayer that will help you Totally Lovin My Eyes

_____

_____

_____

_____

_____

_____

_____

I'M TOTALLY LOVIN MY

Totally Lovin My Voice

Author

Tunisia Osborne

ABOUT THE AUTHOR

Tunisia Osborne

Tunisia Osborne is a native from California. She is an educator, wellness and fitness coach and Loves singing praises to God. She also is a singer ,and songwriter. Her passion is for everyone to be in a loving relationship with God that goes through Jesus and to know His Perfect Peace and Freedom mind body and spirit on their Journey to Wholeness.

Tunisia Osborne@gmail.com

WholeFit247@gmail.com

www.tunisiaosborne.com

TOTALLY LOVIN MY

Voice

By Tunisia Osborne

"And they Overcame him by the Blood of the Lamb, and by the word of their testimony" (Revelation 12:11)

I was in a dark place. God was right there with me. I had just left my ex-husband and left with nothing but my laundry bag, The WORD of GOD, and my purse. I had tried to leave twice. But I cried out to My Heavenly Father to help me in Jesus' Precious Name. I did not want to live a double life. I did not want to keep smiling and pretending I was ok in a marriage that was spiritually, mentally abusive, and dead. So, in a nutshell God brought me out and here I was sitting at the kitchen table not shortly after being delivered from the pit and delivered from evil spirits through Jesus' Precious Name I found myself struggling to read the WORD of God silently.

My Dad was watching me struggle and finally said why do not you read the Bible aloud. It gave me so much peace when he said it. I knew it was My Heavenly Father speaking through my dad, because my dad never really talked to me about spiritual things. I begin to tear up in my heart. I began to read the Word of God aloud. My Voice is coming into agreement with His Word.

As I was reading the Word of God aloud, I noticed I had more comfort, peace, more joy. I began to read the Word of God all the time and I noticed my racing thoughts were leaving, fear gone, my mind regulated, my voice was back. God used His Word to bring me out and my voice as an instrument to help me through.

Reading the Word of God aloud strengthens my faith. "Faith cometh by hearing and hearing by the Word of God." (Romans 10:17) Mind you let me back up and say I couldn't have regular conversations, I couldn't really talk normally, I had the Spirit of fear on me, my mind was racing, thoughts that were not even mine were there but so was God fighting for me.

The Word of God brought me back to life. The Word is living and breathing. (Hebrews 4:12). And it was the WORD of God that brought life back to my Voice. It was in speaking God's Word and coming into agreement with His precious promises for my life is where my voice was rendered free from being silent. Jesus' power saved me, helped me and through the leading of The Holy Spirit empowered me. Your voice matters. Your voice has the power to empower, encourage and uplift. It also has the opposite to tear down and to destroy so please use your voice wisely to Honor and glorify God in all you do by encouraging and uplifting others and yourself.

Remember Death and Life are in the Power of the tongue. (Proverbs 18:21) So speak life into your life and the lives of others. Your voice is powerful. Your Voice Matters. God is concerned about your voice being heard. He loves to hear your voice. He made you speak and listen. Do not let the enemy's lies deceive you any longer. Remember what Jesus said about the enemy, the devil is a liar and the father of all lies. (John 8:44). The enemy tries to silence our voices; he will use anything to do it. Trauma, pain, and fear are the silencers. God has not given us the spirit of fear; but of power, and of love and of a sound mind (2 Timothy 1:7)

We have the Power to regain our voices back through the blood of Jesus Christ the Son of God who bought our freedom with His life, death, and resurrection. We now stand in His Power to empower others. Where the Spirit of the Lord is there is Liberty. (2 Corinthians 3:17) We are More than Conquerors through Him that Loved us. (Romans 8:37) So Let Us Stand Women of God and Let Us Share our stories in our stories (testimonies) is where we will start to love our voices and through the power of the Holy Spirit and in Jesus' Precious Mighty name, we will heal others and ourselves.

So, let me encourage you further Women of God with the following Tips that will help us to elevate Loving Our Voices. This is truly Inspired by The Holy Spirit **(The acronym F.A.C.E.)**

- **FINDING YOUR VOICE**... History-Telling your Story helps you to find your Voice and your voice to take Flight. Finding your voice looks different on everyone. Finding your voice could be sharing your story, singing your story, dancing your story, writing your story, painting your story...preaching your story, and teaching your story. All this will help you find the root cause of why your voice was silent and will empower you to keep sharing your story. This is where your healing will take place and will plant the seeds for others to be healed as well.

- **ACCEPTING YOUR VOICE-** The only way we can accept our voice is when we truly embrace the Voice Giver. God the Creator of our Voice. God gave us our voice to speak up, speak out, empower, encourage, Praise, Sing, and Worship Him. The More you get to know Him who created you and the Voice, He gives you the more you will accept your voice.

- **CONSECRATING YOUR VOICE-** Making sure you surrender your voice to God. Helps you to Honor Him through your words and actions. This allows God to speak through His Words using your voice. There are times we must be silent and be still and listen to God's Voice. Be still and know that I am God. (Psalms 46:10) Make this following verse a part of your affirmation/prayer. "Let the words of my mouth and the Meditation of my heart be acceptable in thy sight Oh LORD My Strength and My Redeemer." (Psalms 19:14)

- **EMBRACING YOUR VOICE-** Trying to make intentional time to cultivate your voice whether it is in writing, in singing, in playing an instrument, and dancing etc. The more you take time to be available for your voice to grow and take flight the more you will embrace it and be comfortable with it.

When you spell out the **Acronym F.A.C.E**. You get Face, and honestly that is what we all must do is to **FACE** our voices. Do not run away from it, do not be silent anymore, do not bury it, do not back down from it and do not be afraid of it. Your voice is beautiful, your voice is empowering, your voice is powerful, your voice has meaning, your voice will change the world. I love your voice already. - Keep pushing forward my Beautiful Women of God. Our Heavenly Father is smiling on us and loves to hear our voices ...Be the Voice in the room and not the Echo...Totally Loving My Voice.

Tunisia Osborne

Devotional

TOTALLY LOVIN MY

VOICE

And they Overcame him by the blood of the Lomb and by the Word of their testimony,and they loved not their lives unto the death

Revelation 12:11

Devotional Totally Lovin My Voice

When we reflect on our testimonies, we each possess a uniquely woven narrative created by our Maker, our Heavenly Father, Jesus Christ, and the Holy Spirit, God. Through our testimonies and voices, God unveils His glory, power, love, grace, justice, loving kindness, wisdom, and much more within us.

PRAYER

Dear Heavenly Father, I am grateful for the testimony you have blessed me with. Thank you for the voice you have provided me. I surrender the parts of my life where I have struggled to embrace my voice—where trauma, others, myself, and even the devil have attempted to silence me. Please aid me in loving my voice as you intended. I praise you and express my gratitude for your response to this prayer, even now, in the precious, mighty, and powerful name of Jesus. Amen.

Tunisia Osborne

Reflection

Totally Lovin My Voice

Write a affirmation for Totally Lovin Your Voice?

_____

_____

_____

_____

What steps will you take to Totally Love Your Voice and use it?

_____

_____

_____

_____

_____

_____

_____

What does that look like?

_____

_____

_____

_____

Reflection

Totally Lovin My Voice

List 3 take aways from this chapter.

_____

_____

_____

_____

_____

_____

_____

_____

Write a prayer that will help you Totally Love Your Voice

_____

_____

_____

_____

_____

_____

_____

_____

_____

I'M TOTALLY LOVIN MY

Totally Lovin My Self-Care

Author

Carmen Hall

ABOUT THE AUTHOR

Carmen Hall

Carmen Hall lives in the San Francisco Bay Area and enjoys writing about personal development for the mind, body, and soul. You can find her inspirational posts on her Facebook page, Morning Star Books, and watch her book videos on TikTok @booktoklovers2. She also manages a Facebook group called @Book Lover's. In her free time, Carmen likes to spend time with her family and connect with nature.

TOTALLY LOVIN MY

Self-Care

By Carmen Hall

As she awakened from her dream there were tears streaming down from her eyes. The emotions behind her tears were soon to follow. Like a quiet flood, the healing from within started to begin and the peace that she felt touched her mind, body, and soul in a most profound way. In a way that she had never experienced before. This was the starting point from which her self-care journey began. She now had the knowledge and revelation of how empowering it is to love oneself.

"Be still and know that I am God." Psalms 46:10 (KJV)

It is in the times of stillness that we can rest and reflect on God's word. These are the moments in which we can receive knowledge revelation and experience the love of God. To see, hear and receive answers to unanswered questions and to find missing pieces to puzzles. What every woman should know is that she is loved. "For God so loved the world, that he gave his only begotten son so that whosoever believeth in him shall not perish but have everlasting life." John 3:16 (KJV).

Loving yourself reflects God's love for you. Looking for love outside of oneself is not necessary. The love that is received outside of self is in addition to what already exists from within. As women we often get lost in the day-to-day activities that life presents to us. We find ourselves trying to prioritize others' needs and desires rather than our own.

The identity that we have consists of numerous factors which include giving ourselves to others. This is something that is natural for most women and for others it is a learned behavior. A woman identifies herself as a mother, wife, girlfriend, fiancée, auntie. These women run households, are employed and the list goes on. The biggest question, however, is who are we outside of these roles? The roles that women play in society, though significant, can also consume a lot of our time, to the point where there is no time to effectively take care of ourselves. It is essential for women to prioritize and create a space to nurture our well-being, through self-care.

What does self-care look like?

Self-care equals self-discovery. It adds value to yourself and consists of exploring what makes you happy. It is making your happiness a priority and implementing those things that make you happy into your life on a regular basis. It could start with something as simple as smelling a rose, if this is something that brings you happiness.

Self-care can be healing, as it is one of the highest forms of love that we can offer to ourselves. As we replenish and invest in our well-being, we can take the band aid off hidden traumas and beliefs that no longer serve us. If you are seeking to find yourself and improve your quality of life, self-care is something that you should consider. It is the gateway to becoming empowered to improve and create the quality of life that you would like to have for yourself.

When we pour into ourselves, we water the seeds of life that are already within us. Self-care comes in many forms and in many ways. It is up to the individual to decide and Invision what that would look like for you.

Here are some key recommended principles to implement into a self-care routine.

S-Start your day with gratitude. Gratitude gives us something to be thankful for. When we are grateful it puts things into a proper perspective and changes our focus into something more positive. Look for things to be grateful for. Do not be surprised when things to be grateful for start to find you!

E-Exercise is good for your overall health. Choose a regular exercise routine that is convenient for your schedule. For example, dancing, walking, or stretching! Exercise is also a great stress reliever.

L-Love your life. Practice loving yourself and others. Life can be challenging. Plan to love your life regardless. The love that we give to others we can also give to ourselves.
Making changes whenever necessary can improve your quality of life's experiences.

F-Fun can bring joy to many circumstances. What does fun look like to you? Find something that excites you. Playing a fun game or going to a concert. Spending quality time with family and friends. Planning fun activities gives you something to look forward to.

C-Care for yourself. Care is a way of providing for your health maintenance and welfare. This includes your mental, physical, and spiritual health. Care is wanting what is best for you. It can be going to the gym, or getting your hair and nails done. Eating healthier, spending time with God. Whatever it is that makes you feel good about being you. Do those things that bring you joy, peace, love, and contentment.

A-Appreciate who you are as a woman. Ask yourself, what are some of the best things about being a woman? Appreciation for ourselves and others around us adds value to our lives.

R-Rest well and schedule time for you. Create a peaceful atmosphere for yourself. A space where you can rest and be comfortable to the degree where you can relax. Free from anxiety, fears and worries and any distractions.

E-Explore new things! Transform yourself by the renewing of your mind. Allow yourself to experience the goodness of God. There is always something new to learn. It is good to be open to learning new things about yourself. Discover what makes you feel good on the inside and do more of that.

I'm totally loving my self-care. Practicing self-care has opened my eyes to new beginnings. It is an exciting way of being. It replenishes, heals, restores, and reveals insights of awareness that otherwise may have gone unseen. It is an ongoing process that has brought value to my life in many ways. It has led me to the path of personal growth and self-discovery.

Women experience stress on many levels. Implementing regular self-care practices is great for your mental health and can reduce stress. With that said, it is my hope that you find some of these self-care practices helpful.

"And he showed me a pure river of water of life, clear as crystal, proceeding out of the throne of God and of the lamb." Revelation 22:1 (KJV)

She begins to thank God for another day, slowly getting out of the bed she reflects upon her dream, and she begins to smile to herself.

Because she wanted to see the beauty of God she decided to go for a walk. During the walk she focused on the sun, sky, and the trees.

Drawing closer to the water, hearing the splashing of the waves made her feel calm inside. There was stillness in the atmosphere as the birds flew by.

Her life was a living testimony of learning to be content in all things. Now she was learning how to love herself.

Carmen Hall

Devotional

TOTALLY LOVIN MY

SELF-CARE

Be still and know that I am God. Take the time to be still and acknowledge God's presence in your life.

Psalm 46:10

Devotional

Totally Lovin My self-care

During your quiet time, allow yourself to practice self-care. I have found that journaling is a fantastic way to start putting your words into action.

When practicing self-care ask yourself these questions.

What am I grateful for?

How can I acknowledge God in my life today?

What is something positive that I can focus on?

What action can I take to create a pleasant experience for myself?

Practice doing those things that bring you joy and happiness!

PRAYER

Dear Lord, thank You for reminding me that taking care of myself is a way to honor the life You've given me. Help me to embrace self-care with love, knowing that I am worthy of rest, renewal, and compassion. Guide me to nourish my body, mind, and spirit, so I can reflect Your love and serve others from a place of wholeness. In Jesus' name, Amen.

Carmen Hall

Reflection
Totally Lovin My Self-Care

Write a affirmation for Totally Lovin Your self-care?

_____

_____

_____

_____

What steps will you take to Totally Lovin My Self-Care?

_____

_____

_____

_____

_____

_____

_____

What does that look like?

_____

_____

_____

_____

Reflection
Totally Lovin My Self-Care

List 3 take aways from this chapter.

_____

_____

_____

_____

_____

_____

_____

_____

Write a prayer that will help you Totally Love Your self-care

_____

_____

_____

_____

_____

_____

_____

_____

_____

I'M TOTALLY LOVIN MY

Totally Lovin My Season

Author

Cynthia Jordan

ABOUT THE AUTHOR

Cynthia Jordan

Apostle Frank Jordan and Apostle Cynthia Jordan have been married for 35 years. We have three children, Michael, Deron, and Kera, and two grandchildren, Michael Jr. and Isaiah. She has served in ministry in many capacities. I was ordained a Prophet at Greater Community Missionary Baptist Church in St Roberts, Missouri, under the leadership of Dr William Boone.

My husband and I served as Pastors of Rhema New Life Ministry in Allenhurst, GA, under the
leadership of the late Apostle Dedra Harvey. Apostle Jordan was affirmed an Apostle in 2019. We were later called to start The Prophetic Connection Inc. in 2015. We are a church where deliverance takes place and souls are saved.

Social media names are Cynthia Jordan and The Prophetic Connection on Facebook
Micynt on Instagram and The Prophetic Connection2015

TOTALLY LOVIN MY

Season

By Apostle Cynthia Jordan

Ecclesiastes 3:1 is a scripture that speaks to the natural rhythms and cycles of life, reminding us that there is "a time for every matter under heaven." This profound truth resonates with us as we journey through different seasons of life, each with its own distinct challenges and blessings. As a sixty-year-old Black woman Apostle in the church, you stand at a unique intersection of faith, wisdom, and life experience. Your journey is a testament to God's faithfulness, and your current season is one of fruition, impact, and continued growth in Christ.

1. Reflecting on God's Faithfulness**

In your life, you have seen the Lord's hand guiding you through many different seasons, from your youth to your current stage. You have witnessed His faithfulness in times of trial and joy. Now, as you enjoy this season, it is an opportunity to reflect on God's faithfulness throughout your journey. Remember the challenges you have overcome and the victories you have celebrated. Reflecting on God's steadfast love strengthens your faith and encourages you to trust Him even more in the season you are in.

2. Sharing Wisdom and Guidance

In your current season, you are a source of wisdom and guidance for others, particularly those in the faith community. As an Apostle, you have been entrusted with a special calling to lead and shepherd God's people. Your years of experience have equipped you with insights that can only come from a life lived in faith. As you navigate this season, take the time to pour into the lives of others, offering mentorship, encouragement, and spiritual guidance. Your journey can inspire and uplift those who are just starting their walk with Christ.

3. Cultivating Relationships

As you embrace the season you are in, focus on cultivating meaningful relationships with your family, friends, and church community. Your presence is a source of strength and inspiration to those around you. Invest time in building deeper connections and offering support to those who need it. This is a time to celebrate the relationships that have grown over the years and to continue sowing seeds of love and compassion.

4. Embracing God's Timing

Ecclesiastes 3:1 teaches us that there is a time and season for everything. In your current season, it is important to embrace God's timing for your life. Sometimes, God may lead you to rest and reflect, while at other times, He may call you to step out in faith and pursue new endeavors.

Trusting in God's timing means being open to His leading and allowing Him to direct your path. Your role as an Apostle requires a discerning spirit to know when to speak and when to listen, when to act and when to wait.

5. Enjoying the Fruits of Your Labor

Your current season is one in which you can enjoy the fruits of your labor. As a faithful servant of God, you have poured yourself into the work of the ministry and have seen the church grow and flourish. This season offers you the opportunity to appreciate the impact you have made and the lives you have touched. Take the time to celebrate the excellent work you have done and the legacy you are building for future generations.

6. Continuing to Grow in Christ

While this season allows you to enjoy the fruits of your labor, it is also a time to continue growing in Christ. As you navigate this phase of life, seek deeper intimacy with God through prayer, worship, and meditation on His Word. The relationship you have built with the Lord over the years will continue to sustain you and guide you in this season. Embrace the opportunity to deepen your faith and allow God to reveal new truths and insights to you.

7. Being a Source of Encouragement

In this season, you could be a source of encouragement to others. Your life story, filled with trials and triumphs, can inspire others to keep pressing on in their own faith journeys. Share your testimony with those who need to hear it and offer words of hope and encouragement to those facing challenges. Your presence in the church and community can be a beacon of light, pointing others to the goodness and grace of God.

8. Remaining Open to God's Surprises

Finally, as you enjoy the season you are in, remain open to God's surprises. While this season may bring a sense of stability and fulfillment, God may also lead you into new and unexpected paths. Trust in His plans and be ready to follow His lead, even if it means stepping out of your comfort zone. Embrace the adventure of faith and allow God to use you in new and impactful ways.

In conclusion, Ecclesiastes 3:1 reminds us that there is a time and season for everything under heaven. As a sixty-year-old Black woman Apostle in the church, you are in a season of enjoying the fruits of your labor, sharing your wisdom, and deepening your relationship with Christ. Embrace this season with gratitude, joy, and a heart open to God's leading. May you continue to be a vessel of His love and grace, bringing hope and encouragement to all who cross your path. I am totally Lovin the season I am in!

Cynthia Jordan

"The beginning of wisdom is this: Get wisdom.
Though it cost all you have, get understanding."
Proverbs 4:7 (NIV)

Reflection
Totally Lovin My Season

Write a affirmation for Totally Lovin My Season

_____
_____
_____
_____

What steps will you take to Totally Lovin your Season?

_____
_____
_____
_____
_____
_____
_____
_____

What does that look like?

_____
_____
_____
_____
_____

"There is a time for everything, and a season for every activity under the heavens: a time to be born and a time to die, a time to plant and a time to uproot, a time to kill and a time to heal, a time to tear down and a time to build, a time to weep and a time to laugh, a time to mourn and a time to dance...
Ecclesiastes 3:1-8 (NIV)

Reflection
Totally Lovin My Season

List 3 take aways from this chapter.

_____
_____
_____
_____
_____
_____
_____
_____

Write a prayer that will help you Totally Lovin My Season

_____
_____
_____
_____
_____
_____
_____
_____
_____

I'M TOTALLY LOVIN MY

Totally Lovin My Myself
In the workplace

Author

Allena Douglas-Braithwaite

ABOUT THE AUTHOR

Allena Douglas-Braithwaite

Allena Douglas Brathwaite is a dedicated servant of God, passionate about sharing His grace, mercy, and miracles. She actively supports outreach ministries, providing for the homeless, single and teen mothers, the sick, and domestic violence survivors. Allena has overcome personal trials, including losing her mother and grandmother, and found healing through her faith. A registered nurse with 30 years of experience, she currently works with the Army Behavioral Health population.

Allena is also a brain aneurysm survivor and advocates for brain aneurysm awareness and domestic violence victims. She and her husband lead the JAB Blessing Bag Ministry, and they are proud parents and grandparents. Allena has attended the School of Prophets and has contributed to three Christian book collaborations.

Facebook: Allena.Douglas-Brathwaite
Instagram: justallena

TOTALLY LOVIN MY

Myself

In The Workplace

By Allena Douglas-Braithwaite

I am delighted to share with you the remarkable journey of faith and service that has shaped my life and ministry over the years. My journey is a testament to God's grace, guidance, and unwavering presence amid life's challenges and victories.

Growing up, I was deeply rooted in my Christian faith, actively involved in church activities, and striving to live a life that reflected the values of kindness, compassion, and dedication. However, despite my outward commitment, I realized there was a profound need for a deeper, more personal relationship with God.

In March 2010, my life took an unexpected turn when I suffered a brain aneurysm while at work. The subsequent medical crisis, including cardiac arrest and brain surgery, brought me face to face with mortality and the reality of God's purpose for my life. In that moment of crisis, I made a vow to God, promising to live a life dedicated to His will if He granted me healing. Little did I know, this was the beginning of a transformative journey of faith and ministry.

It was not an instant transformation. God worked patiently in me, teaching me the importance of prayer, fasting, studying His Word, and serving others with love and compassion. As a nurse with over 30 years of experience, I found my calling as a Behavioral Health Nurse Case Manager for the military. In this role, I encountered intense spiritual warfare, facing challenges, opposition, and even physical threats at times.

I would often try to show everyone I was friendly, helpful and a representative of God's love only to be rejected and to meet opposition and warfare. Once I realized that it was not me that they hated, it was the spirit of God that lived on the inside of me. I stopped taking it personally and learned how to effectively pray, discern and to walk in forgiveness. Despite how I was treated I showed love. The word says, Ephesians 6:12" For we wrestle not against flesh and blood, but against principalities, against powers, against the rulers of darkness of this world, against spiritual wickedness in high places. Knowing this, I kept myself equipped with the Whole Armor of God.

Through it all, I held on to the promise of John 16:33, where Jesus assures us of His victory over the world's tribulations. This scripture became my anchor during the storms of life, reminding me that God's presence and power are greater than any challenge I may face.

My journey taught me valuable lessons about the true meaning of ministry. Contrary to popular misconceptions, ministry is not confined to traditional church roles but encompasses every aspect of our lives. As stated in 1st Corinthians 10:31, whatever we do, whether in our professions or daily tasks, should be done for the glory of God.

One of the scriptures that deeply resonated with me during my journey is James 1:2-8. This passage emphasizes the importance of faith, patience, and unwavering trust in God, especially during trials and temptations. It reminds us that God grants wisdom to those who ask in faith and remain steadfast in their beliefs.

Reflecting on my experiences, I am reminded of God's multifaceted roles in our lives. He is our Advocate, Creator, Provider, and Father, orchestrating all things for our good and His glory (Romans 8:28). As I walk in partnership with Christ, I strive to do my part with excellence, trusting God to work miracles and fulfill His purpose through me.

In moments of adversity or overwhelming challenges, I draw strength from scriptures like Joshua 1:9, Psalm 18:32, and Philippians 4:13. These verses reaffirm God's presence, strength, and victory in every situation, empowering us to overcome obstacles with courage and faith.

The heart of ministry lies in serving God and others with love, humility, and dedication. As we acknowledge God in all aspects of our lives, our daily work becomes a form of ministry, reflecting His love and light to those around us.

I encourage you to embrace your unique calling and ministry, knowing that God equips and empowers us to make a difference wherever we are. Let us walk with faith, trusting in God's promises, and serving Him wholeheartedly in all that we do with blessings and gratitude.

Allena Douglas-Braithwaite

Devotional

TOTALLY LOVIN MY

MYSELF

IN THE WORKPLACE

"Do not conform to the pattern of this world, but be transformed by the renewing of your mind. Then you will be able to test and approve what God's will is—his good, pleasing and perfect will."

Romans 12:2 (NIV)

Devotional

Totally Lovin Myself
In the workplace

It is an honor to serve as an ambassador of God in this world. Let us work for His glory and be a witness to His love and mercy!

- Honor God by doing your work well.
- pray for your coworker.
- Pray when faced with challenges and adversity.
- Be a light in a dark place.
- Be ready to assist your clients and co-workers as needed.
- Treat others as you want to be treated (Luke 6:31, Matthew 7:12).

PRAYER

Dear Heavenly Father,

Thank You for the unique gifts and abilities You have given me. Help me to love and value myself in the workplace, embracing the strengths and qualities You've placed within me. Give me confidence to shine, serve others well, and bring my best to every task. In Jesus' name, Amen.

Allena Douglas-Braithwaite

Reflection

Totally Lovin Myself
In the workplace

Write a affirmation for Totally Lovin Myself In the workplace.

_____
_____
_____
_____

What steps will you take to Totally Love Yourself in the workplace?

_____
_____
_____
_____
_____
_____
_____

What does that look like?

_____
_____
_____
_____

Reflection

Totally Lovin Myself
In the workplace

List 3 take aways from this chapter.

_____
_____
_____
_____
_____
_____
_____

Write a prayer that will help you Totally Love Yourself in the workplace

_____
_____
_____
_____
_____
_____
_____
_____

I'M TOTALLY LOVIN MY

Totally Lovin My Skin I'm In

Author

Leah Sanchez

ABOUT THE AUTHOR

My name is Leah L Sanchez . I'm a Wife , Mother , Sister, Aunt ; Pastor and Friend. My family and I relocated from Brooklyn , Ny and settled in Kinston , NC in 2015 . My passion is working with children with special needs and my online Boutique (Bending Bows Boutique) .

I am under the leadership of Apostle Sherri Ezzell at Ground Breakers Regional Hub . I am currently on a sabbatical seeking the Lord . I sat down from Ministry to work on my self. To realign my walk in faith with the Lord and the assignment for my family and I .

TOTALLY LOVIN MY

Skin I'm In

By Leah Sanchez

Totally lovin the skin, I am in and how God created me. I am a Child of God, Wife, Mother, Daughter, Sister, Aunt, Friend, and Pastor at my local assembly. However, there was a time when I was not comfortable in the skin I was in. When, after a long battle with addiction and deep inner pain, just when I thought I was healed and delivered, the enemy strategically crept into my life. With one swift blow after the next, my life was flooded with crushing memories of childhood trauma, the failure of old and very toxic relationships, and dangling over my head was the struggle of sobriety- a war I had conquered now pressing me to fight again. And, with this, the invitation to isolate, to run and hide in my pain. And, so, I hid under the guise of "Ministry Sabbatical."

Alarming still, during my sabbatical, I became comfortable in the wastelands of my wilderness. I no longer had a desire to do Ministry. I wanted NO part in it. My desire to minister to God's sheep had completely diminished. Furthermore, being asked to pray with people, let alone engage with people, was out of the question. I was dangerously comfortable sitting in the back of the church and being the first out the door before the close of service. I even went to the extent of ignoring and suppressing my gifts and calling, as well as the beckoning of the Holy Spirit, both inside and, eventually, outside of the church. I was no longer comfortable in my skin.

Inattentively, wandering through life and getting the bare minimum done was my only desire and care. I was letting go of everything and escaping all the hurt and failure. Self-protecting and numbing any pain with what pleased me in that moment would help me make it through whatever this was. I was "LIFE-Ing," If that is a word I can use to describe my aimlessness. Chasing after what I thought would mask the void I felt in my heart while my marriage, motherhood, and Ministry drifted off like precious cargo lost at sea.

What once felt like the most important things in my life—the people and places I had held dear and prioritized—became a blur in the distance. No, I was not comfortable in the skin I was in, and although I was pushing everyone away, deep inside my heart, I was screaming out for help. I felt as though I had isolated myself so deeply within my aimless world that no one could hear me, no one could see me... or so I thought.

God was right there waiting for me to let Him in. It brings a smile to my face today because when I let Him in when I got tired of going through the motions and completely surrendered my will, my faithful Father was there to pull me out of the layers of shame and woundedness I had buried myself underneath.

Greater still, the spiritual and physical fatigue and despondency that had once left me flatlined in my faith, like an old garment, were now removed and replaced with His love, glory, and life- God's life, my portion. What grace and mercy He lavished on us.

God met with me in my surrender and made it easy for me to completely lay down my heaviest burdens and place them at His feet. No guilt, no shame, just an overdue meeting between a daughter and her loving Heavenly Father. At that moment, months of attack lifted, and inner healing and deliverance began again without the enemy's interference and schemes. My Lord, Jesus, reminded me of all the promises and prophecies spoken over me. He reminded me that my past does NOT dictate my future; my past is my past. It is finished. I am healed, delivered, and set free.

In this current chapter of my life, I am saved from defeat and liberated from the burden of childhood/adolescent traumas. The enemy could not keep me bound, and his lies were broken off my life! I am walking in a more than a conqueror mentality, Romans 8:28-39. I have shed the weight of old toxic relationships and the generational curse of alcoholism.

I embrace the light of faith and devotion in Jesus, guiding my every step. I am no longer burdened by the chains of the past. I walk forward with courage and gratitude, knowing I am cherished and loved beyond measure! I am still in awe at how my Lord and Savior, Jesus Christ, looked past all my flaws and chose to run after me, just at the chance He could capture my attention and my heart all over again!

Today, I take my journey, yoked with Christ, one day at a time. Learning to live without being easily offended, I yield to the Holy Spirit and follow His leading in my gifting and calling, abide graciously in God's boundless love, and out of His extravagant love flowing through me- live in the beautiful skin I am in! You, too, can begin to love the skin you're in. You were beautifully and uniquely designed. Although life has many twists and turns, you are who God says you are. He can bring you to a place totally Lovin the skin you are in. Do not give up; you have hope and a great future!

Leah Sanchez

"Your beauty should not come from outward adornment, such as elaborate hairstyles and the wearing of gold jewelry or fine clothes. Rather, it should be that of your inner self, the unfading beauty of a gentle and quiet spirit, which is of great worth in God's sight."

1 Peter 3:3-4 (NIV)

Reflection Totally Lovin My Skin I'm In

Write a affirmation for Totally Lovin My Skin I'm In

_____

_____

_____

What steps will you take to Totally Love Your skin your in?

_____

_____

_____

_____

_____

_____

What does that look like?

_____

_____

_____

_____

Reflection
Totally Lovin My Skin I'm In

List 3 take aways from this chapter.

_____

_____

_____

_____

_____

_____

_____

Write a prayer that will help you Totally Lovin My Skin I'm In

_____

_____

_____

_____

_____

_____

_____

_____

I'M TOTALLY LOVIN MY

Totally Lovin My Recovery

Author

Lisa W. Squire

ABOUT THE AUTHOR

Lisa W. Squire

Lisa W. Squire is a dedicated wife and worship leader, who loves serving her community through outreach. Lisa firmly believes that no matter what we experience in life, it's all apart of God's plan to see us through, so that we can be a blessing to others through the word of our testimony.

TOTALLY LOVIN MY

Recovery

By Lisa W. Squire

When I was asked to write about my journey to healing, I thought, who am I? The woman who has had more pain, problems, and baggage than most people. Then I heard the spirit say why not you. All you have been through and experienced, even though it happened to you, most importantly it is for someone else just like you. So, then I began to allow myself to revisit the pain of my past. Why did it take so long for me to get over some things quickly and other things not so quickly? Some things just stuck with me like a body part.

I revisited the why me syndrome, we all have played that role before at some point in our lives. Then came the guilt, the part I played in some of the things I had gone through, such as bad relationships with men whom I trusted and loved, the miscarriages of a child due to severe stress, depression and the use of alcohol to cope with the pain and guilt of it all.

The questions just kept coming, even though I knew God to be a forgiving God and a loving one, why me? Let us face it, all the pain we endure is not just about who did what to us. We often have played a role in that pain as well. As I began to understand myself, I realized the times I stayed in something longer than I should have been. I played a major part in that experience as well. I held on to that victim role. Never wanting to take ownership in my part.

Which had me holding on to unforgiveness, bitterness, the whole pity party. Then to add to everything else I was personally going through I lost my father, who never hugged me nor said I love you in my life to me, but he provided the best life for me.

I became his caretaker until his death, and I loved showing my love for him. It was one thing after another, my life headed in another vicious cycle when losing my brother three months later, then losing my mom less than eight months after him. Three major deaths in one year. Thinking I could not take anything else. I lost my last brother one year after that. I was wounded and damaged! Who survives these kinds of blows in life?

It was not until I got tired of being Prophesied to over and over, about how anointed I was, and how God had so much in store for me. I knew a drastic change had to happen in my life. I was the Only one who could make that change.

The Steps...

First things first, I had to be honest with my pain and rate the level I was at in it. Why had I, let it consumed my life? Why was I wearing it like a liquid bandage with a Fake smile to top it off.

The Second Step I had to work through was forgiving myself and others who hurt me. Even and the current people who had hurt me. Yet, they knew nothing about this pain and how they hurt me deeply.

The Third Step, I had to Repent to God and a few others to make things right along my path to healing. I could not truly repent until I knew what I was repenting for.

The Fourth Step, I had to do was fast and pray to deepen my relationship with God.

The Fifth Step was very emotional for me because I had to cut some people out of my life. Often, we give the wrong people access to us who mean us no good, they love to draw from you but never deposit into you (**Amos 3:3**)

The Sixth Step involved vulnerability, I had to tell someone I trusted dearly, the nature of my pain and problems. Someone who I knew would pray and cover me as I was recovering, my Spiritual Leader.

The Seventh Step was so crucial, I had to Believe I was Loved by God despite everything I had gone through and that I was worth the work that I had to do.

The Eighth Step was I had to write out affirmations about me and read them aloud everyday aloud.

The Nineth Step was I knew I had to invest in My healing process financially by going to therapy, and retreats, my favorite one being The Healing Kitchen with Dr Misty Beards and her wonderful Tribe of sisters, who are now My Tribe of sisters. I found out we all Need accountability.

The Tenth Step I must continually do the work to maintain My Newfound Healing...and you too can make that change! You can heal...I am loving My Healing Process.

"The Lord is close to the brokenhearted and saves those who are crushed in spirit." Psalm 34:18 (NIV)

Totally Lovin My Recovery

Write a affirmation for Totally Lovin My Recovery

_____

_____

_____

What steps will you take to Totally Lovin Your Recovery?

_____

_____

_____

_____

_____

_____

_____

What does that look like?

_____

_____

_____

_____

Reflection

Totally Lovin My Recovery

List 3 take aways from this chapter.

_____

_____

_____

_____

_____

_____

_____

Write a prayer that will help you Totally Love Yourself in the workplace

_____

_____

_____

_____

_____

_____

_____

_____

I'M TOTALLY LOVIN MY

Totally Lovin My Walk

Author

Monee Jarmon

ABOUT THE AUTHOR

Monee Jarmon

Monee' is a passionate advocate for empowering young women, driven by her deep faith in Jesus Christ to help them elevate their lives through professional etiquette and personal development. With years of experience in modeling, fashion, and coaching, she blends her industry expertise with compassionate, faith-based guidance. Monee' is committed to inspiring confidence, elegance, and purpose in her clients, ensuring they step into every room with the grace of God. Her mission is to transform not just appearances but mindsets, equipping women with the tools they need to succeed in all aspects of life while honoring their faith.

TOTALLY LOVIN MY

Walk

By Monee Jarmon

Empowering Women to Embrace Their Identity and Confidence Through Modeling and Faith.

In the fast-paced world of fashion, where trends come and go like the changing seasons, finding one's footing can be a daunting task. As I reflect on my journey, I realize that my walk – both on and off the runway – has been a catalyst for personal growth, empowerment, and faith. Through my experiences in the modeling industry, my journey of self-discovery, and my commitment to empowering others, I have discovered the transformative power of embracing who I was created to be and helping others do the same.

My journey began with a dream – a dream to grace the catwalks of the world's most prestigious fashion capitals while teaching others how to navigate through their modeling careers. As a young girl, I was captivated by the glamor and allure of the modeling world, but I never imagined that I could be a part of it. Growing up, I struggled with confidence and self-esteem issues, feeling like I did not fit the mold of what society deemed beautiful or desirable. However, as I began to immerse myself in my faith in God, who he has called me to be, and the world of fashion and modeling, I realized that beauty comes in all shapes, sizes, and colors.

With each runway show, photoshoot, and casting call, I grew more confident in my own skin. I learned to embrace my unique features and celebrate the beauty of diversity. Modeling became more than just a career; it became a journey of self-discovery and empowerment. Through the lens of a camera, I saw myself in a new light – as a strong, confident African American woman of faith capable of anything she set her mind to while keeping God first.

But it was not just the external validation of the fashion industry that fueled my confidence; it was also the internal transformation that took place as I found my identity in Christ. Growing up in a Christian household, faith has always been a central part of my life. However, it was not until I faced the challenges of the modeling industry that I truly began to understand what it means to find my identity in Christ.

In a world that often values superficial beauty over inner character, it can be easy to lose sight of who we are and whose we are. But through prayer, meditation, and reflection on God's word, I began to see myself through His eyes – as a beloved daughter, fearfully and wonderfully made.

I realized that my worth and value are not determined by my appearance or accomplishments, but by the unshakeable love and grace of my Creator.

With this newfound confidence and sense of purpose, I felt called to empower other women – especially young women – to embrace their "true identity" and walk with confidence. Thus, I founded Invoking Change LLC, my model and confidence coaching company, where I combine my passion for modeling with my commitment to faith-based empowerment. Through workshops, seminars, and one-on-one coaching sessions, I help women discover their unique beauty, cultivate confidence, and unleash their full potential.

One of the cornerstones of my coaching program is teaching women how to walk – not just on the runway, but in life. Your walk is more than just a physical movement; it reflects who you are and what you believe. By teaching women how to walk with grace, confidence, and purpose, I empower them to embody their true selves and embrace their God-given identity.

One of the most rewarding aspects of my coaching journey has been witnessing the transformation that takes place in the lives of the women I mentor. From timid and insecure to bold and empowered, I have seen firsthand the power of embracing who you were created to be. Whether it is conquering the runway or navigating the challenges of everyday life, my clients leave my coaching sessions with a newfound sense of confidence and purpose.

In conclusion, my journey of loving my walk – both as a model and as a woman of faith – has been a testament to the transformative power of embracing who we were created to be. Through my experiences in the modeling industry, my journey of self-discovery, and my commitment to empowering others, I have learned that true beauty and confidence come from within. By walking with purpose and faith, we can inspire others to do the same and leave a lasting impact on the world around us while invoking change.

Monee Jarmon

"Trust in the Lord with all your heart and lean not on your own understanding; in all your ways submit to him, and he will make your paths straight."
Proverbs 3:5-6 (NIV)

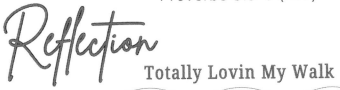 

Totally Lovin My Walk

Write a affirmation for Totally Lovin My Walk

_____
_____
_____
_____

What steps will you take to Totally Lovin My Walk?

_____
_____
_____
_____
_____
_____
_____
_____
_____

What does that look like?

_____
_____
_____
_____
_____

Reflection

Totally Lovin My Walk

List 3 take aways from this chapter.

_____

_____

_____

_____

_____

_____

_____

_____

Write a prayer that will help you Totally Lovin My Walk

_____

_____

_____

_____

_____

_____

_____

_____

_____

Declarations

For The Total Woman Within

FATHER THANK YOU FOR CREATING ME WELL.

IT IS BECAUSE YOU HAVE DESIGNED ME TO HEAL AND MAKE ME WHOLE.

TODAY, I EMBRACE YOUR GLORIOUS DESIGN FOR MY LIFE.

I DECLARE, NO LONGER WILL I LINGER IN THE SHADOWS OF MY PAST.

NO LONGER WILL I LIVE IN THE VOICES AND OPINIONS OF OTHER!

I DECLARE THAT I AM FEARFULLY AND WONDERFULLY MADE.

I AM HEALED FROM ALL OF MY DIS-EASES, AND I NOW BEGIN TO WALK IN THE PURPOSE AND DESTINY YOU HAVE IN STORE FOR ME.

I DECREE MY HEART HEALS FROM ALL SELF-GUILT AND SHAME, AND I NOW EMBRACE AND ACCEPT YOUR FORGIVENESS TOWARDS ME.

I AM CREATED

TO TOTALLY LOVE ME!

TOTALLY SUCCEED IN ALL AREAS OF MY LIFE.

TOTALLY FORGIVE ME AND OTHERS.

TO TOTALLY SEE LIFE THROUGH A NEW PERSPECTIVE.

TODAY I DECLARE THAT I

TOTALLY LOVIN MY VOICE,

TOTALLY LOVIN MY EARS,

TOTALLY LOVIN MY LIFE,

TOTALLY LOVIN MY JOURNEY,

TOTALLY LOVIN MY TREASURE WITHIN,

TOTALLY MY WALK,

TOTALLY LOVE MY JESUS,

TOTALLY LOVIN MY SISTERHOOD,

TOTALLY LOVIN MY PAST,

TOTALLY LOVIN MY FUTURE,

TOTALLY LOVIN MY DETERMINATION

TOTALLY LOVIN MY START OVER,

TOTALLY LOVIN MY UNIQUENESS,

TOTALLY LOVIN MY LUXE LIFE,

TOTALLY LOVIN MY RECOVERY,

TOTALLY LOVIN MY IDENTITY,

TOTALLY LOVIN MY BODY,

TOTALLY LOVIN MY SELF-CARE,

TOTALLY LOVIN MY SERVITUDE

TOTALLY LOVIN PERSPECTIVE,

TOTALLY LOVIN MY SISTERHOOD,

TOTALLY LOVE MY SEASON,

TOTALLY LOVIN THE SKIN I AM IN,

TOTALLY LOVIN MY STEP-BY-STEP WALK,

TOTALLY LOVIN MY EYES,

TOTALLY LOVIN MY PERSPECTIVE

TOTALLY LOVIN MY HEALING PROCESS,

TOTALLY LOVIN MY TRAVEL EXPERIENCES,

TOTALLY LOVIN MY BOUNDARIES

TOTALLY LOVIN MY STORY

TOTALLY LOVIN MY DIFFERENCES

AND TOTALLY LOVIN MY WINS.

Color or write on this page things you are rising and to bloom.

Rise THEN Bloom LIKE THE Lotus

Write a letter to yourself

Bonus

FREE DOWNLOADABLE EBOOK

TOTAL WOMAN WITHIN PRAYER & AFFIRMATION

www.tlmmpublishing.com

TLMM PUBLISHING YOUTUBE CHANNEL

MOMENTS WITH THE TOTAL WOMAN WITHIN
PODCAST/VIDEO/WEEKLY INSPIRATION

- TLMM PUBLISHING

- MEET THE AUTHORS OF TOTAL WOMAN

  WITHIN